ISLAND KEEPERS

ISLAND KEEPERS

ALLISON MITCHAM

LANCELOT PRESS
HANTSPORT, NOVA SCOTIA

ISBN 0-88999-383-1
Cover design: Joan Sinclair
Published 1989

LANCELOT PRESS LIMITED
Office and production facilities located on Hwy. 1,
$\frac{1}{2}$ mile east of Hantsport, Nova Scotia.

ACKNOWLEDGEMENT
This book has been published with the assistance
of the Nova Scotia Department of Tourism and Culture.

Contents

Acknowledgements

to the administration of the Université de Moncton for *dégrèvement* and the *Conseil de recherche* for several grants; to my colleagues for their support; to Phyllis Roy, secretary of the department of English, for typing my final draft;

to Dr. Stephanie Mitcham for reading and correcting the final draft of the manuscript;

to Dr. Peter Mitcham for several of the drawings and maps;

and to the following individuals and institutions: my publisher and his wife, Bill and Isabel Pope, for their interest in my subject from the start; the staff of the Public Archives of Nova Scotia (Halifax) — particularly, Philip L. Hartling, microfilm archivist, J.B. Cahill, manuscript archivist, and Margaret Campbell, photo and map archivist; J. Mahony Plummer, public services librarian, Faculty of Law, Dalhousie University (Halifax); Graham McBride, curatorial assistant, Maritime Museum of the Atlantic (Halifax); Dr. Robert Morgan, director, Beaton Institute, College of Cape Breton (Sydney); Patricia Kennedy, chief of pre-confederation archives, manuscript division, Public Archives of Canada (Ottawa); Jeffrey Murray, map archivist, Public Archives of Canada (Ottawa); Anne-Marie Pépin, cartographic and architectural archives division, Public Archives of Canada (Ottawa); Howard C. Brown, archivist, Provincial Archives of

Newfoundland and Labrador (St. John's); Marguerite Syvret, Société Jersiaise (Jersey, Channel Islands); Soeur Yvonne Chiasson, Head Département d'anglais, Université de Moncton; the staff of Mount Allison University Library (Sackville); the New York Public Library; Naomi Mitcham; Donald P. Lemon, prints, drawings and photographs, New Brunswick Museum (Saint John); Mr. and Mrs. Charles E. Haliburton and Miss Gail Hersey, Admiral Digby Library and Historical Society (Digby); Ruth Miller, Reference Librarian, Mount Allison University Library; Doug Pope.

Foreword

This is an account of days long past. It is about the years when Nova Scotia was a power to be reckoned with, when British and American vessels vied with one another to harvest the then seemingly inexhaustible resources of her offshore fishery, and when markets of the world snapped up all the coal, the grindstones, the timber and the ships her people could produce. This period — the just under one hundred years from 1784 to 1873 — was shaped by men of nerve and grit and imagination. Joseph Frederick Wallet DesBarres, Samuel Cunard, and Joseph Howe all helped to determine and control events of this period. Connected with these remarkable men and their many ventures were others almost equally significant in their own time, although less well known in ours. Among these were several members of the Dodd family of Sydney, Cape Breton, colorful and controversial individuals around whom the events in this book revolve.

After the introductory ANTECEDENTS, the point of view of this narrative is Philip Dodd's; its immediate setting, Sydney in 1873, just after Dodd's return from an eighteen-year stint as superintendent of the Humane Establishment on Sable Island; its nature, retrospective, episodic, and reflective; its intent, to humanize and elucidate this man's life and times, his work and relationships.

Since the various aspects of this book may at times cause some readers — particularly those who, like myself, have a strong alternative focus on precise chronology — to wish for an ordered table of dates and facts to refer to, I have provided just such a sequential and objective reference to follow and supplement Philip Dodd's necessarily oscillating and subjective viewpoint. Conventional footnotes would not, I believe, render so satisfactory a service to the average reader at whom this book is aimed.

Yet all this is not to intimate that the narrative is based on anything other than a close scrutiny and analysis of relevant correspondence, logs, memoirs, reports, and other historical data. It simply calls attention to the fact that this work is an interpretation of the available material, its sequences ordered by the author's understanding of her subject's responses to his environment.

I

Antecedents

How could two brothers from one of the most influential Cape Breton families of their time choose to live on the two most feared islands off their native coast? What, one wonders, could have induced them to exchange the comforts and prestige of the big Sydney house on "Judge's Corner" for the dangers and loneliness of Scatarie and Sable, where conditions were said to be worse than those on the world's most notorious prison islands? What vision of fulfilment or escape prompted first James and then Philip Dodd to take on the arduous and nerve-racking duties of superintendents of the Humane Establishments of such infamous trouble spots?

* * *

James Richard Dodd and Philip Sherwood Dodd were born to wealth and privilege. They and their nine brothers and sisters were sponsored by the most important people of their native Cape Breton and by a good many luminaries from the outside world as well. Governors, ships' captains, generals, merchants and visiting dignitaries hovered around their bassinets and cut short business, military and naval engagements to appear promptly at their christenings. The exact dates of their births, their inoculations for smallpox, and their bouts with mumps, measles, and whooping cough were meticulously recorded in the family Bible, as if these youngsters had been fledgling princes and princesses. Even the location (frequently Halifax) of their confrontations and confinements with these childhood maladies was duly noted.

Such devoted attentions were not difficult to understand when one checks the impressive list of appointments which the children's father, Archibald Charles Dodd, received during their early years, and is reminded of other important and advantageous associations which were formed prior to their births.

Archibald Charles Dodd's rise to power in Cape Breton and his longstanding dominance there, coincides almost exactly with the years of that island's separation from the rest of Nova Scotia between 1784 and 1820.* In 1787, Dodd, a man then in his mid-forties, arrived in Halifax from England. He was scarcely off the boat before he was on the governing council in Sydney (as recording clerk without stipend) at the behest of then Lieutenant Governor Joesph Frederick Wallet DesBarres. In short order he was president of the council and manager of Des Barres' Cape Breton affairs during the frequent and extended absences of this versatile, erratic, talented and much travelled gentleman.

By 1787 DesBarres had signed over a parcel of land bordering on both Great George and DesBarres Streets so that Dodd could build a house suitable for entertaining the prominent people he was increasingly involved with. For although Sydney would never rival Louisbourg, the French capital of Cape Breton during the early part of the eighteenth century, as a model of elegance, the new territorial administrators still expected to maintain themselves in circumstances befitting their elevated positions.

When Dodd did built his own establishment he chose a location further from the barracks and closer to what was to be the center of the town. Understandably, he patterned it after English country houses he had known. His home was not

---

* In 1784 the province of Cape Breton was created (as was the province of New Brunswick) with its own governor and judiciary. However, in 1820, due to mismanagement by a series of military governors, Cape Breton was reannexed to Nova Scotia.

12

Founding of Sydney, Cape Breton, 1785
Lt. William Booth delin: watercolour on paper, 37.5 x 68.6 cm, w-1710. The New Brunswick Museum/Le Musee du Nouveau-Brunswick, Saint John, Nouveau-Brunswick.

indeed as grand as his maternal grandparents' hall at Tofthouse, Northumberlandshire, which, according to rumor, he had been done out of by his younger brother while on an extended continental tour, but it was a large and substantial house by early Sydney standards.

Meanwhile, Dodd had been courting a young lady of means and prominence, Susannah Gibbons, only daughter of Richard Gibbons, the new province's Chief Justice. Clearly, Susannah would be the ideal wife for him: well-connected, suitably endowed both by nature and fortune, and young enough — fourteen, according to church records; sixteen, by one family estimate — to bear him the large family which prestigious gentlemen of his era were expected to beget.

On July 8, 1788, Archibald and Susannah were married. Just over two years later, on August 20, 1790, their first child, Charles William Macarmick was born. His sponsors were Lieutenant-Colonel William Macarmick, then Governor of Cape Breton, and William Cox, captain of the twenty-first regiment — fitting guardians for a well-born child in a garrison town. Thereafter, at regular intervals of two to three years (up to 1814) ten more children were born. Of these,

James Richard, the future first superintendent and keeper of Scatarie Island, born December 13, 1795, was the third, and Philip Sherwood, destined to be the fifth superintendent of Sable Island, born July 16, 1806, was the eighth.

As the family grew, the father's sphere of influence expanded. In 1790 he was appointed acting collector of customs (an office he subsequently held for nine years). In 1801 this position was extended and A.C. Dodd was named Collector of Provincial Revenue for the Island of Cape Breton — "more immediately and particularly of the Import Duty upon rum and other spiritous Liquor." Overlapping with this appointment was his position (beginning in 1792) as Post Master of Sydney. In 1802 he was named Superintendent of Coal Mines (an office he held until 1806). In 1803 he became Deputy Surveyor General of Woods on the Island of Cape Breton under Sir John Wentworth. In 1806 he was appointed the fourth (and last) Chief Justice of Cape Breton, an office he had held temporarily on several occasions and which he was to hold — on and off — until Cape Breton was reannexed to mainland Nova Scotia. Periodically, he was called on to run the province of Cape Breton on his own.

The office with which A.C. Dodd was most publicly associated was that of Chief Justice — and it was from this position that he was several times suspended — notably in 1807, and again late in 1814 when he was called to London to give an account of himself and his doings. He at first refused to answer this latter summons, stating that at the advanced age of seventy-two, he was not up to a mid-winter Atlantic crossing. However, he did make the trip the following summer. During his stay in London he presumably set his critics' minds at ease: he was not only reinstated as Chief Justice, but a few years later (in 1820), when Cape Breton was reannexed to mainland Nova Scotia, he was rewarded for his apparently invaluable services with a pension equaling his full salary — for the rest of his life. If those who gave the pension thought cynically that they could afford to make this generous-seeming offer because Chief Justice Dodd was then 80 years old and could hardly be expected to live much longer, they were caught out in their reckonings. He went on . . . and on — for another eleven years

— and even then his demise was due to no ordinary cause. He was tossed from his horse.

Although Chief Justice Dodd's vigor, his seemingly irrepressible zest for life and his determination to participate in many of the activities which had occupied him during the years of his greatest prominence (from 1787 to 1820), were indeed noteworthy, his wife's presence of mind and strength of character were equally remarkable. After all, during the late eighteenth and early nineteenth centuries, men of A.C. Dodd's calibre and station — many, long-term survivors like himself — were to be seen elsewhere in Nova Scotia. Prominent among them was Dodd's dynamic mentor, Colonel DesBarres himself, who not only lived to be over one hundred, but was a going concern almost until his death. Later there were others — men like Amos Seaman of Minudie, dubbed the "Grindstone King," who demonstrated a similar sort of sustained enthusiasm for living and a seemingly tireless pursuit of individual goals.

Wives of such successful and energetic men tended to live in their husband's shadows. Overburdened in their youth by yearly confinements for childbirth, and neglected in middle life, they were apt to subside into lassitude, ill health, and early graves. Susannah Dodd was *not* such a woman, despite the difficulties she had to cope with.

Mother of eleven children and hostess to most of the elite who resided in or visited Sydney, she had to adjust to a good many traumatic occurrences from which neither money nor position could protect her. When she was still a very young woman — in 1794, the year before James was born — her parents and only brother, Richard, had, on their way back from England, been taken prisoner by the crew of a French frigate.* For a long while there had been no news of their whereabouts . . . though, eventually, notification of her father's death in prison. Then, her brother Richard, after his escape to England in 1796 and his return home, had been hard to get along with. He seemed always to have a chip on his shoulder.

---

* The French Revolution had begun the previous year and the French forces, fired with revolutionary zeal, renewed their efforts against the English with whom they were at war.

When he had read law with Archibald there had been all those terrible arguments. The situation between them had not improved with time. She had hoped after Richard had been appointed Attorney General for the province (in 1808) that the tensions would ease. They had not. Instead, her husband and brother had been so objectionable with one another that they had both been threatened with suspensions from office. She had been sick of all the uncertainty — fed up with the acrimony and back-biting. Why, even the Reverend Cossit, their first vicar, had entered the political controversies, and then been obliged to leave town because he had become so helplessly embroiled in them.

In addition to such confrontations, Susannah had had trouble adjusting to the boys' early departures from home. James was off to serve as midshipman in the Royal Navy at fifteen. Then had come the capture and imprisonment of both James and Edmund (two years James' junior) during the war of 1812. Edmund had been freed and had returned home in 1816, but James had been absent and incommunicado for so long after the war that everyone had assumed he was dead. Yet Archibald, she realized, had never quite given up hope of his son's return. He had, for instance, included James in the will he had made several years before his death. Indeed the postscript to this document had upset her so much that she knew she would remember it to her dying day: ". . . And my further will is as to the share of my beloved son, James Richard Dodd, whom I have not seen or heard as being alive for some years, that should he not be returned or not known to be alive when my said property is to be divided amongst my children, as aforesaid, that his share shall not then go to his heirs, but shall merge in my general property, and be divided equally, share and share alike, among the rest of my said children or their heirs."

As if all these family troubles had not provided heartache and uncertainty enough, Susannah Dodd had had to cope with the worry of her husband's recall to London to explain supposed irregularities — or at least his highhanded-ness — in his management of colonial judical business.

As she had waited and watched, unable herself to resolve any of these affairs, her sharp and satiric mind must have increasingly pondered the idiosyncrasies of fate. When her coachman drove her to the fine house which her brother had completed shortly after his return from the French prison, she doubtless considered the peculiar twists by which marble from the ruins of the old fortress of Louisbourg, brought originally from France at great cost to grace the establishments of its newly transplanted rulers, had then been installed in the residence of one of their successors, an heir of their enemies who had himself been held captive in old France. There was no accounting for such complex ironies.

Even the changes in the town had been unsettling — the way she'd watched it deteriorate. The winter before her marriage — the year Colonel DesBarres had saved the townsfolk from starving by paying out of his own pocket for provisions to be hauled in overland from Arichat — had been the beginning of the slump. Colonel DesBarres had (according to Archibald, who should have known) spent his last penny and borrowed more in this humanitarian gesture, and had then not been reimbursed. What had the British government expected? Did the parliamentarians think he should have let the population of Sydney starve? Apparently!

DesBarres' hasty departure from Sydney, she recalled, had been a signal to a good many of the original settlers to get out of town too. Next time a crisis occurred, they guessed, no one would be willing to provide for them.

The following summer, 1788, there had indeed been a grand flurry of activity when the Prince of Wales, William Henry (afterwards William IV), had sailed into Sydney on the *Andromeda* and remained in town several days. She and Archibald had thoroughly enjoyed the party Lieutenant Governor Macarmick had thrown in honor of his Royal Highness and the ceremony at the water's edge when the harbor had been named Prince William Henry Sound.

However, the lift provided by the royal visit had lasted no longer than the new name for the harbor. By the next season both were all but forgotten.

By the year of James' birth, more than half the homes of Sydney were empty, many in ruins. Susannah had looked back over the scrapbook she had kept and reread the facts she had copied down from a report she had found on Archibald's desk:

17

"There are 27 inhabited dwellings, 17 uninhabited, 27 in ruins and 14 public buildings. The population is about 150 to 160. (May 1795)"

Briefly, after the turn of the century, the town had had an infusion of new blood — nearly all Scots. She remembered that August day in 1802 when she had taken the children down to the harbor to watch the ship anchor and the emigrants file off. She recalled the vessel's odd name, the *Northern Friends*. The boys had kept pestering her about its port of origin. They had wanted to count the newcomers as they disembarked. They had, she remembered, counted more than four hundred when she had said that she couldn't stand up a moment longer. John, then not quite a year old, could not walk yet, and she could still recollect how exhausted she had felt, holding that great squirming lump of a ten-month-old in her arms.

Just a few hours on the wharf with the six children, watching and counting, and she had had enough. What about the poor emigrant women she had seen? How, she had wondered, would their pale children survive the coming winter? Who would provide for them when the fiasco of Colonel DesBarres' rescue mission was still fresh in most people's minds? Anyway, who had the resources? Not the governor, not the small garrison, not even the handful of well-to-do families like the Dodds and the Gibbons.

She was still not sure what had happened to all of them. Some had gone to work in the mines, a few had tried to farm, and quite a few more, she had heard, had found their way to Halifax where some had starved and some had received help.

The caustic wit for which Susannah Dodd was remembered seems to have been much exercised during these difficult years — and thereafter. Perhaps it was her defence against all the events she could not control or explain — the deterioration of the town, Archibald's difficulties with the establishment, her father's death in the French prison, her brother's enforced stint in the army of the Revolution after his capture (Richard in a French uniform — unbelievable!), and her mother's storybook escape from the Château de Roncourt clutching that small circular box of polished wood which was supposed to contain a fragment of the 'True Cross.' The ridiculous and unsettling image of her middle-aged, matter-of-

18

fact and staunchly Church of England mother escaping from a French château with the aid of the enemies of her country — a daring American and the French and Catholic mistress of the château — seemed so incredible that Susannah would never have believed a word of it is she had not heard the story from her mother's lips and actually held the strange little box which the Frenchwoman had promised would guarantee her mother's safe return to her faraway home.

Her mother had seemed to forget this adventure rather quickly, being reluctant as the years passed to discuss the unusual events. Ultimately, it was Richard who seemed most influenced by his enforced sojourn in France. Although on the one hand he continued to complain about the fact that he, a British gentleman, had been coerced into joining the French Forces, on the other, he went out of his way to surround himself with French influences. He built his house in the French manner from Louisbourg stone. He married the only eligible French-speaking young lady from the Sydney district — Anne Ingouville, daughter of Philippe Ingouville of Jersey who had been one of Colonel DesBarres' friends and an early grantee like their own father. Finally, he called his eldest son Napoleon!

Such behaviour was typical of Richard — contradictory as the island's winds. Poor Anne! . . . However, Susannah couldn't help thinking that Richard was a lot like their father who, though protesting that he despised the French, in the same breath proclaimed Colonel DesBarres, another Frenchman,* the most talented of men and his best friend.

Archibald too had often been contradictory and inconsistent, but he was not bad-tempered like Richard. Archibald's conflicts with his peers were certainly wearing for a rational observer, but generally she judged them inconsequential. She felt in her bones that he would be all right. Although he was always having to go off somewhere to explain himself, he seemed to say the right things, whatever they were. He invariably bounced back.

---

* DesBarres' birthplace is unknown. Some say he was born in France, some Switzerland.

Observing life from the top of the social ladder had made a difference to Susannah's perspectives. She had witnessed plenty of slips and a lot of wobbling on the top rungs as the climbers shifted their weight too suddenly to one side or the other, but she had rarely seen anyone fall off and be unable to get up again — that is, until her father's final disaster. However, that, a wartime capture, could hardly be equated with any earlier difficulties.

She still remembered vividly the turmoil in her parents' home just six months prior to her marriage when her father had been told that he was to be suspended from his office by the Lieutenant Governor and Council. He had subsequently rushed to Quebec to see Lord Dorchester, who had not been very helpful. She did not know exactly what had happened over the next few years — her marriage and the birth of her first two babies had claimed most of her attention — except that her father had been recalled to England. He had had a long wait there — so long in fact that he had seemed reluctant to hurry back to Cape Breton when he was reinstated as Chief Justice in 1793. He had taken a whole year winding up his affairs in England. Susannah had often speculated about how different things might have been if her father had been more prompt about returning to his Cape Breton duties. There would, for instance, have been no capture by the French frigate *Tribune*.

Yet mostly Susannah Dodd seemed to have pondered the amazing resilience of the great and near great. Colonel DesBarres — a man who capped a lifetime of remarkable and eccentric feats by dancing on a tavern table top at his 100th birthday celebration — was probably the most dramatic example amongst her immediate acquaintances. Removed from office as Lieutenant Governor of Cape Breton in 1787, he slipped away to the Island of Jersey to avoid imprisonment for debt before resurfacing to manage his estates. After almost twenty years of this semi-retirement, he had stepped back into the limelight as governor of Prince Edward Island, a position he had held for nearly a decade. That he was 83 when he assumed this appointment was perhaps its most surprising aspect.

Who then could fathom the vagaries of the British establishment in meting out colonial positions! Clearly, she saw, no one should try to understand the criteria or he or she would go mad, and perhaps even end up by committing suicide like that poor super-sensitive Lieutenant Governor Armstrong. But that had been more than half a century before, when the French still controlled Cape Breton — or "Isle Royale" as they had called it — and the English governed the rest of old "Acadie" from Annapolis.

Finally, with Susannah, it was the everyday matters — the comings and goings of the children in particular — that sometimes got her down. Once James and Edmund had gone off to sea, there was no controlling the family as she had done when the first four youngsters were small.

Susannah Dodd did, however, according to everyone else's reckoning, hold her household together until her children were all launched. Then, as her great, great granddaughter has related, "she betook herself to her bed, from which she criticized her neighbors, dictated to her relatives, and set everybody right in the matter of history or disputed quotations. She was wont to assert her right to a legal mind and good judgment on the claim that she was 'the daughter of a Chief Justice, the wife of a Chief Justice, and the mother of a Supreme Court Judge (Edmund).' "

Yet it is doubtful whether even the perspicacious Susannah ever guessed which of her own and Archibald's prestigious acquaintances would be most influential in determining the lives of their children. Sir John Wentworth did not seem among the foremost contenders. He had indeed had business dealings with Archibald concerning the forests of Cape Breton, but apart from these, it was difficult near the turn of the century to imagine any other significant impact that Sir John was likely to have on the Dodd family.

Nevertheless, the connection turned out to be important — although roundabout and long-term. Sir John's eventual and long-standing impact on the lives of James and Philip Dodd had indeed nothing at all to do with woodlands. It was instead a result of his insistence on starting a life-saving establishment on Sable Island, that notorious sand crescent near which so many fine ships had foundered since the sixteenth century at least.

Now the original idea for setting up this station had not

21

been Wentworth's, but John Howe's.* Nevertheless, it had been Sir John's endorsement of Howe's idea and his persistence in following it through which were responsible for getting the project underway.

Wentworth alternately begged and battled for support. The British government was not greatly interested. While prominent Englishmen had long been notable for dispensing the sort of good advice which Thomas Crawley had given Archibald Dodd in 1797 — "set your wise heads together and form some plan for the settlement of your Island (Cape Breton); or in all human probability it will remain in the savage state that it is in at the present until the Americans walk in and make a better use of it than we have done" — they had, at the same time, shown notorious reluctance to back schemes which involved spending money.

That offshore Maritime islands were particularly vulnerable to attack, as well as worth holding on to, had been demonstrated again and again throughout the preceding century in the struggle over Cape Breton Island and the Canso Islands. Eighty years earlier Governor Philipps and Lieutenant Governor Armstrong had tirelessly spelled out the dangers of not defending these islands. They had been right.

Sable Island, it was becoming clear, was just another such troublesome spot, where indeed there had already been, apart from wrecks galore, a number of unpleasant confrontations with American fishermen, pirates, and wreckers. The difficulties had been publicized in Boston and in Halifax, as the following newspaper item indicates:

One Jesse Lawrence, who lived on the Isle of Sable, to receive wrecked people, and to carry on the seal fishery, was attacked by people from Massachusetts, who landed there and wantonly pillaged and destroyed his house and effects, and then compelled him to leave the island. He received some compensation from governor Hancock and his council, which still left him a

---

* John Howe was a printer, editor and the father of Joseph Howe. Joseph Howe worked with his father and acquired many of his ideas and abilities from this association.

sufferer. — Boston, 1 January, 1789.
(Reprinted in the *Nova Scotia Gazette*, February 10, 1789.)

Yet when Wentworth referred to this and other such tales of disaster pertaining to Sable Island, British officials brushed them aside. Wentworth, they were beginning to think, was turning out to be another overly zealous governor. The English parliament had preferred to have Sir John's energy channelled into getting the pines out of colonial forests for Royal Navy masts instead of into this wild scheme of installing a life saving station on the shifting sands of a godforsaken island.

Their attitude seemed reasonable at the time. After all, many members were quick to point out, nowhere else in the entire civilized world was there a "Humane Establishment" such as the one Sir John advocated placing on Sable Island in 1801. Besides the estimated initial expenditure of £900 for maintaining the seven men and their families (the minimum number, Wentworth felt, who could do the job of patrolling the then 30-mile-long island), together with the complicated logistics of setting up such a station on this desolate, sandy outpost, seemed insurmountable. Why, the whole notion was ridiculous! Sir John himself had drawn attention to some of the problems — the evil reputation of the island, for instance, and the difficulty of finding a suitable person to put in charge.

Wentworth had indeed warned against bringing in only families of the lower classes because he thought that they would be subject to moral deterioration if left to themselves. At the same time he admitted that these were likely the only kind of people who could be induced to live on Sable Island, since they were apt to be tempted solely by an offer of "Pay and Provisions." The chief problem, then, according to Wentworth, was to find an exceptional individual to put in charge of this operation; otherwise, he predicted, it would fail. Such a man, he stipulated, had to be "a Gentleman of Respectability and Character, who is also a Man of Business, or at least a good Accountant."

On a remote island where provisions were to be brought in only twice a year at most, and where, even in an emergency, there was little hope of getting help from the mainland, the superintendent of the Humane Establishment had to be extraordinarily resourceful and commanding. He was to be an absolute ruler; his authority, like that of a ship's captain, unquestioned. Moreover, he was likely to be under more constant pressure than a ship's captain, since there was never the cheering prospect of arriving in port. The superintendent, his men, and their families were to be anchored permanently on an unprepossessing sand bar, some 110 miles out from Cape Canso, the nearest part of the Nova Scotia mainland, and 170 miles from Halifax, the city from which the rescue station was to be administered.

That Wentworth persevered with his scheme, setting up his Humane Establishment despite lack of funds, and installing just such a practical "Gentleman" as he had described, is now a well-established fact. With a few hitches now and then, the venture over the years proved to be more successful than Wentworth in his most optimistic moments could ever have wished. Its success, indeed, was so apparent that thirty years later, another enterprising and forceful Haligonian, Samuel Cunard, was pushing for additional establishments of the same sort in comparably treacherous locations. One of the most notorious of these spots — said in fact to rival Sable Island as the "graveyard of the Atlantic" — was Scatarie Island, a rocky triangle some fifteen miles northeast of Louisbourg. It was here that James Dodd, gentleman and seafarer, was established in 1835 on the joint recommendations of his brother Edmund, member representing Sydney in the Nova Scotia House of Assembly, and Samuel Cunard, shipping magnate and lighthouse commissioner, to initiate Scatarie Island's Humane Establishment. And it was partly James' undertakings on this island which eventually launched his brother Philip into a comparable, though more established, position on Sable Island.

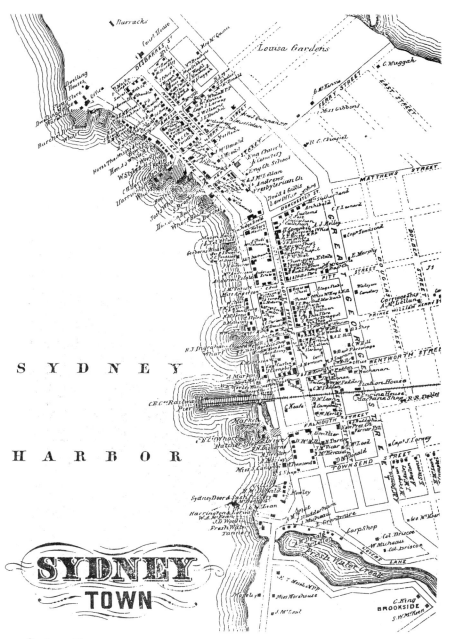

Sydney Town   From Church's map of Cape Breton (1864)

Hon. Edmund Dodd
(PANS N-4640)

II

Reflections

"The Steamer *Lady Head* arrived at Sydney, C.B. on Tuesday last from Sable Island . . . . She had on board Philip Dodd, Esq. who for the long period of 18 years had been Governor of the Island, and had not been off the Island during this time. He intends remaining here. His successor has not been appointed."

What a luxury to be able to sit back and read the newspaper so soon after it rolled off the press! No waiting for weeks or months for the arrival of the supply ship! No chance either of the paper being soaked by the surf breaking into a lifeboat running ashore from the *Daring* or the *Lady Head!* And today there had even been a few lines about his own return . . . . Eighteen years on a shifting sand bar more than 100 miles offshore, and that was all they could find to say!

Philip began to think back over all those years and the events which had led up to his going to Sable Island. He had plenty of time now to reflect. For the first time in his life he was free to sit back if he wished, to put the happenings of the past into some sort of perspective. As they had occurred, he had certainly had no sense of there being any sort of pattern. He had simply, it seemed, been propelled by necessity from one situation to another. Now he felt inclined to scrutinize the facts and see what he could make of them.

Most of the other governors of Sable Island, and a good

many lightkeepers elsewhere too — James, for instance — had never had this opportunity. Hard-pressed financially and often ailing physically, most had died in harness or been reduced to begging the government to support them in the last years of a "miserable existence." These were indeed the very words which Hodgson, one of his predecessors on Sable, had used in filing a petition with the government for support during retirement. Philip had come upon what he had assumed was the rough draft of this letter among papers which several former superintendents had left behind at the Principal Station.

Neither Hodgson, nor any of his other predecessors — except McKenna, of course — had, as far as he could determine, been as fortunate as Philip himself. They had not had substantial land holdings, legacies or savings to fall back on after their return to the mainland, nor had they had a competent and family-minded brother like Edmund to look out for them. Edmund's connections in the House of Assembly in Halifax and with the Sydney establishment too had been Philip's and James' salvations on more than one occasion.

Edmund and James seemed always to have been at the center of his life. Edmund, who was so like their father — a controversial and argumentative lawyer-politician, an eager committeeman in Sydney and Halifax, father of a large family . . . ; James, who had gone to sea and to war long before he, Philip, could remember, had been the focus of family speculations year after year, been given up for dead, and then amazed everyone by resurfacing just about the time Edmund had been elected to the House — only to vanish again among the rocks and mists of Scatarie Island. In Philip's eyes Edmund was, first and foremost, practical and conservative; James, heroic and romantic. Philip had always imagined himself somewhere in between these two in temperament and capabilities.

Although Edmund had gone to sea early — at precisely the same time as James — and had even been imprisoned during the war of 1812, he rarely spoke of this experience, seemed never to have been traumatized by it. When he, Philip, had as a youth begged for details, Edmund had merely searched out an old clipping from the *Acadian Recorder*,

written by a Nova Scotian who had been taken captive. Tl.
young man's article, describing at some length the route
marches, the imprisonment in cold, cramped and fetid cells,
the uncertainty . . . , had been smuggled back to the Halifax
newspaper which had published it. The account had then been
saved, he guessed, by the families of countless young men —
many of them mere boys like Edmund and James — who had
undergone similar experiences.

"It was much as he described," Edmund had remarked
with reference to the clipping. However, he had spoken with a
finality and authority which, Philip had assumed, had
precluded further discussion.

Edmund's return to Sydney in 1816 had changed
Philip's life. Edmund, a lithe nineteen-year-old in a mate's
uniform, had seemed a handsome and commanding presence.
Appearing older than his years, he had seemed destined even
then to be a person of importance. The impressionable ten-
year-old had dogged his elder brother's footsteps.

Even when Edmund had packed away his uniform and
settled down to study law, he had seemed worth watching. He
had been less glamorous, perhaps, than in his naval uniform,
but he had still been fascinating. Purposeful and self-assured,
he had soon taken his place as their father's ally against the
increasingly powerful forces in Halifax which had been intent
on reannexing Cape Breton.

Philip had heard a lot of talk during this era which had
been over his head. What had stayed with him had been his
impression of the forcefulness of Edmund's personality.
Edmund had become increasingly a power in the family and in
the community. It had been obvious that he was to be his
father's political successor and the new head of the family.

And although Edmund and their father, together with
their associates from Cape Breton's first families, had by 1820
lost their battle to keep their province separate from Nova
Scotia, the coalition had nevertheless remained powerful and
in control of many regional affairs. The Dodds, the Bowns, the
Leonards, the Archibalds, the Hall Clarkes, the Ritchies, the
Gibbons, the Crawleys . . . had been determined to hold onto
the safe and lucrative positions which they considered
rightfully theirs — in some cases, sinecures which would

29

'm in the social and financial niches which they had
\stomed to filling.
\stoms officers and mine managers; as harbor
revenue cutter captains; as lawyers, doctors and
......ans, as consular agents for the Americans . . . their
places had been struggled for and held on to. As justices of the
peace, as judges and political representatives of all sorts, they
had held sway. Philip could see now that newcomers had
either joined their tight family coalition or been excluded.

Yet increasingly there had been few significant
newcomers. Sydney had remained poor. There had not been
enough positions for the offspring of the first families, let alone
outsiders. There had been increasingly bitter competition for
any new places which had been considered sufficiently
prestigious for sons of good families to bother with.

If Sydney had flourished as Governor DesBarres had
hoped, there would have been work enough for everyone. But
by and large, the mines, the farms and the fisheries had been
mismanaged. Even the garrison had shrunk over the years in
numbers and prestige, so that now, save for a few officers on
half pay, there were few indications of its former prominence.
Even Saint George's, formerly the garrison church, had been
rebuilt with stone from Louisbourg shortly after Philip had
gone to Sable Island.

As Philip saw in retrospect, the first families had spent
most of their energies looking out for themselves and their
offspring and enjoying the good life. When there had been no
sinecures left in Sydney, the heads of these families had
extended their influence to nearby settlements — to Lingan,
Bridgeport, Menadou,* Cow Bay** and Louisbourg. Even on
offshore bases — on lonely outposts such as Scatarie, Sable
and Devil's Islands — Sydney's elite had established their kith
and kin when responsible positions with adequate stipends
offered.

* * *

---

* Menadou is now generally written as Main-à-Dieu.

** Cow Bay is at present known as Port Morien.

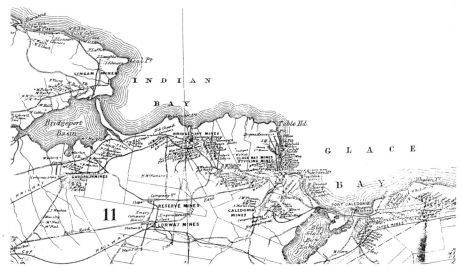

Bridgeport and vicinity   From Church's map of Cape Breton (1864)

When he had first gone to Bridgeport, Philip had felt a real sense of relief in escaping from the immediate orbit of Edmund, contentious Uncle Richard, and their powerful and aggressive friends and enemies in both Sydney and Halifax. In Bridgeport he had his new job, his young wife, and, in quick succession, two beautiful children: a boy, Philip Sherwood, and a girl, Ellen Susannah — Elley, as she was called almost from the first.

There had, of course, been the christenings at Saint George's, as well as other family gatherings in Sydney, but the focal point of his life had shifted from there so that nearly everything he did had revolved around his small family in Bridgeport . . . that is, until the death of his son.

For, if Bridgeport had been the setting for Philip's emancipation, it had also been the site of his life's (and Susannah's) great tragedy. After that chill December day when young Philip, not yet 14, had died in the mine explosion near the cliff face, life had never quite returned to normal. Its more tranquil and predictable patterns seemed to have been forever shattered. From then on it was as if both he and

31

Susannah had steeled themselves for other out-of-the-blue catastrophes. Only through his work — especially at sea, away from the places which reminded him most strongly of the boy — could he sometimes forget. Susannah, at home, had not been so fortunate: she had had too much time to reflect.

In the years following their son's death Philip had thought it only fair to give up his life at sea. If he had not been away so much of those four years before young Philip's death, perhaps things mightn't have happened as they had.

However, it had taken time before a suitable position offered. Every year spent at sea fits a person less and less for anything on land, he reflected for perhaps the hundredth time.

So the opportunity to live ashore again, when it did arise, had not been a conventional one. The offer, superintendent of Sable Island, had meant a break for them both with everything that had gone before. And he had to acknowledge, now anyway, that his reasons for taking it had not been only Susannah's despondency and his own feelings of guilt, but a crisis, or a series of impending crises, aboard the fisheries schooners . . . . That, topped off by his reaction to James' life, and death, on Scatarie.

III

Troubles in the Fisheries

"... history teaches that the commercial prosperity and
naval power of every maritime state had risen, by slow
degrees from the prosecution of the fisheries, in which
seamen were trained, and hardy defenders nurtured . . . .

. . . The richest fisheries in the world surround these
coasts . . . ."

— from a petition to "the Queen's most excellent
majesty by an influential group of merchants and
inhabitants of Halifax and other parts of Nova
Scotia." (2nd September 1852)

"Throughout the Gulf, there is no fishery so valuable as
that on the Cape Breton shore . . . ."

— Colin Yorke Campbell, commander H.M.S.
Devastation Halifax, 10 November 1852.

There had, of course, for centuries been troubles — indeed,
disputes of monumental proportions — concerning the
fisheries of Nova Scotia in general, and those of Cape Breton
and the Canso Islands in particular. Philip realized now that
the difficulties he had experienced were part of an extensive
power play which had been going on for centuries, though with

increased stakes since the French founding of Louisbourg and the extensive settlement and independence of New England. But, while he had been involved in them, Philip had been concerned with the day to day difficulties rather than the historic perspectives.

How, Philip had wondered, could a person become so firmly enmeshed in contentious proceedings and equivocal political manoeuverings when all he had intended was fulfiling the seemingly straightforward demands of his job? He had thought his instructions absolutely clear: in keeping with the treaty of 1818, he was to patrol the waters around Cape Breton, apprehending foreign fishing vessels which had strayed within three miles of the coast (or within the bays cut off by dominant headlands).

Like most Maritimers of his class, Philip had long understood the necessity for upholding this law, aimed at controlling the illegal activities of the huge numbers of American fishing captains who routinely violated the treaty. The Americans had long dominated the best inshore fishing grounds and safest harbors along the Atlantic coasts of British North America. They came ashore where and when they pleased, caught bait and dumped offal on whim and even dried their codfish on stretches of shore which they expropriated for this use. In all this, everyone knew, they had shown a total disregard for the rights of the native inhabitants, the legal proprietors.

It was just that defending these rights was no easy matter. The American fishermen were everywhere and there was no way of stopping them without having an extensive fleet of fast and well-armed vessels to intercept and charge them. Neither the impoverished provincial government nor the British parliament seemed able to find funds sufficient for this purpose. Even when vessels such as the *Sylph*, and later the *Responsible*, the *Halifax* and others were commissioned for this purpose they had been ill-equipped to deal with the Americans.

Besides, the local people were usually of little help in catching the intruders. Frequently they were in cahoots. Too many ordinary Nova Scotians benefitted from the illegal foreign presence: some worked on the American boats for better pay than they could get on their own; and some received contraband, goods they could never hope to acquire legally for so reasonable a price.

Philip had been naive enough to take the job at its face value. First as seizing officer on the *Sylph* and later as master of the *Responsible* he had pursued the lawbreakers single-mindedly. A sort of marine policeman, he had acted with a seaman's disregard for the complexities of politics ashore.* Why, he wondered for perhaps the thousandth time, had he been constituted so differently from Edmund, who, like their father, had mostly seemed to sense well in advance which way the political winds would blow and trim his sails accordingly?

---

* For a more detailed view of the fisheries disputes from Philip Dodd's point of view see Appendix D.

CAPE BRETON

MIRA BAY

MAIN-A-DIEU PASSAGE

SAVA

GREAT SHAG ROCK

MAIN A DIEU

GRANDFATHERS
COVE

MAD
DICK
ROCK

PETER MITCHAM
1988

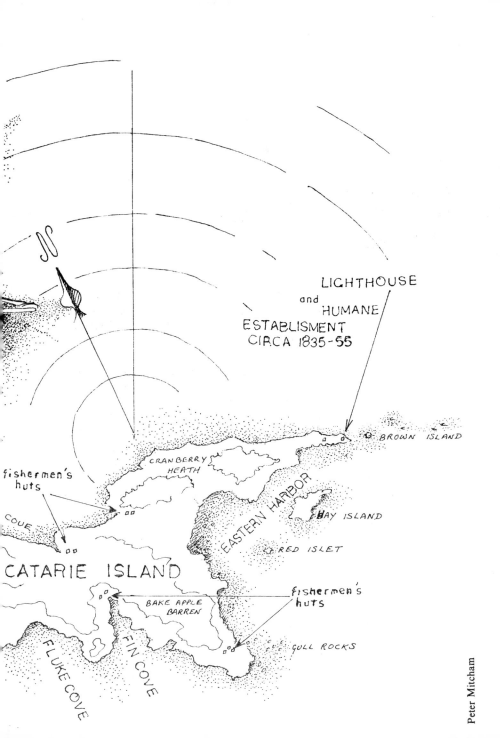

LIGHTHOUSE
and HUMANE
ESTABLISMENT
CIRCA 1835-55

BROWN ISLAND

CRANBERRY HEATH

fishermen's huts

COVE

EASTERN HARBOR

BAY ISLAND

RED ISLET

CATARIE ISLAND

fishermen's huts

BAKE APPLE BARREN

GULL ROCKS

FLUKE COVE

FIN COVE

Peter Mitcham

IV

Scatarie Island:
unyielding rock triangle
1829-1855

". . . it (Scatarie) offers a most excellent station for fishermen. One thousand families might there establish their dwellings, and fish from their boats on productive ground, within call of their houses."

"This island (Scatarie) being usually the first land made by vessels from Europe to any of the colonies eastward of the Bay of Fundy, and from the common occurrence of vessels being ahead of their reckoning, when steering to the westward, the first news of its propinquity being often given by the roar of its breakers or the concussion of its rocks, shipwrecks are of frequent occurrence, and few places on the coast of Northern America more obviously call for the precaution of a light house."

— Thomas Chandler Haliburton, *An Historical and Statistical Account of Nova Scotia* (1829)

* * *

"Thus it appears that there are soundings sufficient to have prevented those numerous and fatal shipwrecks that have strewn the shores of the Island of Scatari [sic] with graves."

— Captain Henry Wolsey Bayfield, *The St. Lawrence Survey Journals* (August 15, 1844)

When Judge Haliburton had sat at their father's table expounding on the threats Scatarie Island posed to shipping and the advantages it offered as a fishing base, the assembled members of the Dodd family had listened politely and nodded absent-mindedly. It had seemed that this island could be none of their concern. Their father was long past an age when any sort of development on Scatarie might have interested him; Edmund, though already embroiled in local politics, had not yet been elected to the House, and had, apparently, no inkling that such an isolated and infertile piece of real estate might have future economic and political significance; James was still absent — heaven only knew where; and Philip himself had been too young, too unformed as yet, to have taken more than a superficial interest in his elders' conversations along these lines. Besides, his thoughts had been elsewhere, on his own adult life which was about to begin.

It had been later — after the publication of the Judge's *Historical and Statistical Account* . . .; after James' return; after the spate of shipwrecks on Scatarie in the early thirties; after Edmund's election to the House; and after his own removal to Bridgeport — that the family's attention had been diverted to this island. By then the focus of much of the rest of Sydney was also riveted on this forlorn spot.

However, it had not been Scatarie Island's potential as a base for a new and thriving fishery which had worked on people's imaginations. Despite the rundown state of the town and the impoverishment of all but its most prominent and independently wealthy citizens, not a single townsman had, it seemed, given a thought to the Judge's idea of establishing 1,000 families on Scatarie to fish cod. Apparently no one had been interested in hearing about the fortunes which had been made in Louisbourg a century before from this offshore fishing station — and with less than half the number of men the Judge had proposed sending out. Consequently, no one had dreamed of how establishing a fishery of such magnitude might make everyone in Sydney — possibly everyone in Cape Breton — well-to-do.

Instead, it was the island's other claim to importance — as the first landfall off the northern coast of Nova Scotia, the landmark most captains steered for, and often ran aground on when approaching the Gulf of Saint Lawrence from abroad — that was on everyone's mind. In the early thirties the town was abuzz with stories of shipwrecked sailors, starving and ragged women and children, battered corpses and rich cargoes which the sea had thrown up indiscriminately upon the island's rocks.

A number of Sydney captains had been obliged to pick up survivors from the wrecks, and they had brought home boatload after boatload of destitute human beings to be billeted upon the town's residents. The situation had seemed unbearable from the beginning — and it had gotten worse. So many Sydney residents could scarcely afford to feed and clothe their own families. What were they to do with all those hungry and half-naked strangers?

By 1834 even Philip, with most of his energy channelled into his new responsibilities at Bridgeport, had still not been wholly able to avoid confrontations with the victims of Scatarie shipwrecks and their rescuers. Both seemed to be everywhere he went. Some of the newcomers had walked to Bridgeport to apply for work at the mines.

Even in the old family house in Sydney there had been no escape from the subject. Edmund, intent on keeping his newly-won seat in the House, had talked of little else when he was home. There had to be, he and his friends proclaimed, a house of refuge in Sydney, funded by the provincial government, for the survivors of local shipwrecks. Edmund had gone on and on about this project and about the trouble he had taken to put before his peers in Halifax claim after claim on behalf of Sydney residents who had helped the Scatarie survivors: Daniel and Bridget Shea; Drs. Grey and Haire; eight captains who had filed a joint petition for nearly £300 . . . The catalogue had seemed endless.

The provincial treasury, Edmund had kept saying, could not continue to pay out such exorbitant sums for the maintenance of victims of one particular trouble spot. There were, after all, a good many other notorious places in the main shipping lanes. Sable and the Seal Islands were two of these and had had almost as many wrecks as Scatarie. Still, these other islands, despite their dreadful reputations, were, as Edmund had never tired of pointing out, not such a drain on the province. The difference between Scatarie and these others was that they had Humane Establishments whereas Scatarie had none. These establishments, through their salvage operations and the good managements of their super-intendents, had cut down immeasurably on the losses — and, Edmund had noted, on Sable, had sometimes even turned a profit.

Bearing these facts in mind, then, Edmund and the most progressive of his Halifax and Sydney colleagues had pushed for a Humane Establishment and a lighthouse on Scatarie Island.

Promises of support had even come from Canada,* the destination of a good many of the vessels wrecked on Scatarie. Since the early thirties an increasing number of immigrant ships bound for Quebec had foundered on the rocks surrounding this island. Yet, perhaps more memorable for official minds than the deaths of countless poor immigrants had been the loss on these same rocks of a troop transport, the *Leonidas* in 1832. Not only had all the troops perished, but large amounts of copper coins, destined to replenish military coffers, had gone down with them.

The loss of the *Leonidas*, Philip saw in retrospect, was the sort of marine disaster which had called for concerted government action. The fuss over this vessel's loss had been — as either Charles Leonard or H.W.Crawley (he could not recall which) had noted at the time — comparable to the furor raised more than thirty years earlier over the wrecking of the *Francis* on Sable Island. The *Francis,* another military transport, had also carried valuables — the effects of Edward, Duke of York, valued at £11,000. And as Leonard or Crawley had remarked somewhat acidly, the wrecking and total loss of military and royal property had certainly seemed to lend great impetus to plans for setting up a Humane Establishment on Sable Island.

---

* In pre-confederation (pre 1867) times, Lower and Upper Canada — later Quebec and Ontario — were referred to as Canada.

41

Perhaps, he had continued, the *Leonidas* disaster would hurry up plans for a similar rescue station on Scatarie.

Then in 1834, when one disaster after another had occurred on Scatarie Island, the disgraceful story of the wrecking of the *Fidelity* and the frightful plight of her passengers had circulated widely and called attention dramatically to the crucial need for immediate government action regarding this newly-notorious place.

* * *

In the spring of 1834, about the 10th of May, the brig *Fidelity*, bound for Quebec from Dublin with 183 immigrants, had struck the rocks of Scatarie. Captain Clarke had managed to land all his passengers on the island where, for a brief while, they had thought themselves safe and thanked God for their deliverance.

Their feelings of relief and gratitude had been short-lived. No friendly inhabitants had come forward to welcome them. Instead, for three days they had wandered through bogs and brush looking for help and failing to find any.

The wretched immigrants had soon realized that here was terrain bleaker and more unproductive by far than the land they had left behind. Here indeed was a wilderness starker and colder than any they could have imagined. Shrivelled berries clung to wiry stems near the ground, half hidden in lichens where patches of snow still lingered. A few dead fish, half eaten, lay upon the rocks. An eagle wheeled above them.

In the course of their wanderings the survivors had learned that they were stranded on an island, roughly seven miles long and three miles wide, and that a strait of at least two miles separated them from the nearest mainland. The only protection from the cold and damp was in several unoccupied fishing shanties which they had come upon. Each of these could accommodate only three or four people at a time. Yet these tiny huts had saved the wanderers. Here they had been able to make fires to dry their sodden garments.

More importantly, the smoke had drawn attention to their presence. The inhabitants of the nearest settlement, Main-à-Dieu, just across from the west end of the island, spotting the smoke, had decided to send several fishermen out to investigate.

The trouble was that the ice had been neither in nor out. It was instead in that treacherous in-between state where a man could not count on walking on it, as he frequently could in mid-winter; nor could he hope to launch a regular fishing boat. Under ordinary circumstances no one would have ventured out among the ice floes. However, the spirals of smoke attested to some unusual occurrence.

The only thing to do, the Main-à-Dieu fishermen had realized, was to take a crew with a small boat. Where the ice held, the men would walk, dragging or pushing the boat: where there was open water, they could climb aboard and row. In this way, they would, with luck, reach the island. They had done it before — but they would have preferred never to have done it again.

Upon discovering the survivors of the *Fidelity*, the men of Main-à-Dieu set about ferrying them — a few at a time — back to the mainland. The villagers took in the newcomers reluctantly, feeding and clothing them as best they could but resenting the drain on their own meager resources. A week more with the burden of these extra mouths to feed, they grumbled, and they would all be able to starve to death together.

It was the end of winter, before the fishing season began, before the gardens started producing. Rations were always short in spring. This year was no exception.

The villagers had dispatched a boy to Sydney, telling him to make haste along the post road. The authorities there had to be told of the disaster. They had to send a vessel, or conveyances of some sort, to take the refugees out of Main-à-Dieu. Three passengers had already died from the ordeal.

While they waited the villagers congratulated themselves that they had succeeded in getting all the immigrants off the island .... at least that was what they assumed .... now the men of Main-à-Dieu felt that they could turn their attention to the wreck. They would salvage what they could. They deserved some compensation.

The fishermen of Main-a-Dieu had worked day and night at the wreck, determined to get off all they could before official salvagers arrived to lay claim to the contents of the

Fidelity's hold and cabins. Coins, and other valuables which would not rot, the men of Main-à-Dieu buried hastily on the island. Summer and fall, during fishing and hunting seasons, would, they reckoned, be soon enough to dig them up again. Then, safe in their shanties, with nosy officials and pathetic immigrants long since gone, they would be able to sort through the booty and divide it at their leisure. The best of the clothing and blankets they kept for their own immediate use and their families', taking them as replacements for all they had given to the shipwrecked immigrants.

It was when they were thus engaged that the men of Main-à-Dieu came upon three more survivors — two women and a girl — who had been eking out an existence on the island for the three weeks since the shipwreck. They had taken shelter in one of the shanties and had lived on fragments of dead fish washed up on the rocks.

* * *

If the fishermen of Main-à-Dieu had regarded their illegal salvaging of the *Fidelity* as just compensation for saving and taking care of the brig's passengers, members of the comfortable upper crust of Sydney and Halifax were appalled at what had happened. Yet what could they do except push with more vigor for the setting up of some sort of government-sponsored and controlled humane establishment and light station on Scatarie Island.

In Sydney, Philip remembered, the Leonards, the Archibalds, the Hall Clarkes, the Crawleys, the Bowns, the Ritchies, the Gibbons and the Dodds — the first families, in fact — had agreed on the need for a legitimate institution on Scatarie to preserve life and property. What they were divided over was the man to put in charge of the light and rescue station. One of their own, certainly, but should he be Edward Bown or James Dodd?

Philip recalled how hot under the collar Edmund had been — and understandably so — about the petitions got up on Edward Bown's behalf while he was absent in Halifax. Twenty of Sydney's most prominent citizens had signed the first one, and more the second. Charles Leonard and Uncle Richard had been among the signers. Leonard's signature could have been no great surprise. The Leonards and the Bowns were connected by marriage like the Dodds and the Gibbons. What had angered Edmund, and presumably James too, was that Uncle Richard had signed Edward's petition.

This was perhaps why, Philip reflected, James had, about this time, dropped his second christian name — Richard, after his patron Richard Stout,* it was true, but also after Uncle Richard Gibbons — replacing it with Raymond, an adaptation of his godfather's surname. This was scarcely an illogical move, Philip had thought, in view of Uncle Richard's treachery and considering that James' first name had been given in honor of the same man — their father's old Jersey Island friend, the prestigious merchant and trader, James Remon. However, it had been a clear indication, Philip could see in retrospect, that James had quietly and finally severed the last connection between himself and their Uncle Richard. Yet because James had made no fuss, most people had not even noticed: The initial "R" was the same for both names, and James was still the name he went by.

Edmund had, of course, won and James, not Edward Bown, had gone to Scatarie. In contrast to their parents' time, decisions — even those govering Cape Breton's affairs — were being made in Halifax, not Sydney. Edmund, since being elected to the House, had made the necessary connections. He had, for instance, made friends with Samuel Cunard, and even Philip had known then that few people in the 1830s had more clout than Sam Cunard in matters pertaining to lighthouses.

Cunard, as everyone in the province knew, was not only a lighthouse commissioner. He had his hand in nearly every commercial venture anyone could mention. Since most of these involved shipping, it was obvious that Sam Cunard had a vested interest in making the coast of Nova Scotia and the sea lanes as safe as possible. It was common knowledge that he had trading vessels dispatched throughout the world to buy up and distribute all sorts of commodities — tea and whale oil, molasses and rum, coal and biscuits. His ten gun brigs

---

* Richard Stout of Sydney held early coal leases and later took over management of all G.M.A. properties in Cape Breton. He had Sydney's first seagoing vessel built (in 1797).

delivered the mails.

Cunard, as Edmund had told Philip time out of mind, had had plenty of first-hand information about the places where his vessels were most likely to founder. He had, Philip had been told, personally visited Seal Island in 1831 when one of his ships had run aground there, and had scarcely rested until a lighthouse was operating on this trouble spot later that same year.

Samuel Cunard's visit to Seal Island and his quick and purposeful response to the hazards he had observed there was, as Edmund had remarked approvingly, typical of the way he operated. He was famous, Edmund had gone on, for getting his information first-hand by travelling to whatever part of the coast of Nova Scotia claimed his attention, and then returning home to Halifax to pressure his business and political associates to take the sort of action he thought necessary. If this were not sufficient to gain his objectives, he did additional lobbying on his yearly visits to London. Edmund had clearly been filled with admiration. Sam Cunard, he had noted, operated much as their father had, though in a wider sphere and with more success. He had an old-fashioned, Benjamin Franklin sort of drive and buoyancy.

Whether the destination was the wildest or the most civilized, Cunard did not seem to mind, Edmund had reported enthusiastically. He found sea voyages stimulating. The pitching deck, the creaking stays and shrouds, and seamen busy about the deck or aloft in the rigging were, Edmund had noted, among Cunard's favorite sights and sounds. Philip had thought he detected a nostalgic tone in his elder brother's words. Did Edmund miss the life at sea?

When, therefore, there had been mounting controversy in the papers and in the House about Scatarie as a marine hazard at least as treacherous as Seal Island — which in turn was said to rival Sable Island — who better to look into the situation than Samuel Cunard? And who more qualified to assist him than Edmund Murray Dodd,* member of the Legislative

---

* Edmund Dodd had also invested in shipping, though briefly and in a small way compared to Samuel Cunard. In 1842 he had had the *Wanderer* built in Sydney, but he had sold this vessel within a year of its construction.

46

Assembly from Sydney Township, son of the well-known and influential Cape Bretoner, A.C. Dodd; and brother of James Dodd, who had so recently (during the shipping season of 1835, and the two subsequent seasons) distinguished himself for his courage and good management in masterminding rescues on Scatarie Island.

Yes, Philip reflected, Sam Cunard and Edmund had had a good deal in common — their driving ambition, their love of the sea, even their ages — give or take a few months. Philip had had the distinct impression that they had both enjoyed their excursion to Scatarie, had found getting away briefly from their business and domestic responsibilities a lark.

James had been 'baching' on the island — living as simply as possible, making do, as he had since Catherine's death four years earlier. They had been, for a few days, three old bachelors together — though, as James had told him later, Cunard and Edmund had acted as exuberant as ten-year-old boys let out of school for the summer. Small wonder they had been enthusiastic, James had later remarked with unaccustomed sharpness to Philip, since they had been paid £50 each for this trip — £20 more in total than he and his crew had received two years earlier for risking their lives in the lifeboat off Scatarie for the entire 1835 shipping season.

From the time they had agreed to undertake the mission, there had been no doubt that both Sam Cunard and Edmund had been really determined to establish a light station on Scatarie. Doing so had been in the personal interest of each — a top priority indeed.

If they had failed to do their homework on the island, and had subsequently failed to convince their own House of Assembly and the other Houses (in Canada, in New Brunswick and in Prince Edward Island) to support a light here, Edmund had stood a chance of losing his seat. Even Philip had known that voters in Sydney had been strongly focused on the outcome of that visit.

Charles Leonard of Sydney proper and Thomas Bown of North Sydney had both been fed up with the amount of travelling they had had to do in order to assess duties on cargoes which had been battered against this formidable rock and its surrounding shoals. The Archibalds and the Hall

Clarkes, with their immense shipping interests, had perhaps been even keener than Charles Leonard and Thomas Bown on a quick and satisfactory resolution to the many problems associated with Scatarie wrecks. And, increasingly, everyone connected with the mines had clamored for assurances that their coal would not end up on the shoals of the most notorious troublespot on the Cape Breton coast.* Since nearly all the vessels which carried coal from the Sydney, Bridgeport, Cow Bay and Lingan mines had to skirt Scatarie coming and going, every voyage up or down the coast was hazardous.

Sam Cunard had had a personal interest in both the coal and the ships. During James' second summer on Scatarie — in 1836, the year of Elley's birth — Sam Cunard had brought his entire family to Sydney for the opening of a rail line from the coal pits to the docks. With the increased wealth he envisioned from an upsurge in coal production here, combined with the stepped-up speed and efficiency in getting this special product onto waiting vessels, the chief remaining weakness in the marketing and distribution appeared to be the treacherous shoals off Scatarie Island.

Small wonder, Philip had thought, that both Sam Cunard and Edmund, on their return to Halifax, had reported that a lighthouse should be built on Scatarie "without delay," and that, because of the exposed location, it ought to be "of substantial and improved construction." They had further stipulated that Scatarie was to have a revolving light, together with "Keepers' Houses and Store Houses and Accommodations for Shipwrecked Persons." Edmund had told Philip later that when Sam Cunard had consulted Maynard** and Tidmarsh**, the estimate for building the lighthouse alone had been £1,500. No wonder the House had looked for support outside the province!

Cunard and his associates had decided that the Scatarie light should be fueled by whale oil. They had argued persuasively that seal oil, though cheaper, threw a weaker light, and that Scatarie was a station where, whatever the cost,

---

* With the possible exception of St. Paul's Island.
** The other lighthouse commissioners.

the best available fuel should be burned. Though the logic of such an argument seemed indisputable, Philip had always wondered secretly just how much Sam Cunard's considerable investment about this time in whaling vessels had influenced this decision.

There could be little doubt, however, that the lighthouse had helped. Philip himself had counted on its friendly beacon. Certainly the number of wrecks had dropped dramatically after its installation. There had never been another dreadful year like 1834. Of course there had been unavoidable accidents in dense fog or driving snow or with vessels caught out in their reckonings. And, because the wrecks had been fewer, more thought had been given to the reasons why some vessels had continued to founder.

James in particular had had opportunities to speculate about these disasters. He had had the advantage over others of on-the-spot observation, the chance to talk to the victims and note the exact tides and weather. He had indeed formulated a good many theories about the wrecks which had occurred during his superintendency.

The difficulty, Philip had found, had been getting James to divulge this information. James had never been a great talker — and Philip imagined that in his daily log James had confined his jottings to single-sentence weather observations.

Whatever his verbal shortcomings, sea captains who had come a cropper on Scatarie — even the crustiest of mariners — had waxed enthusiastic about James' exertions on behalf of themselves, their crews, their passengers and cargoes. And in all his own voyages — hundreds of them, he supposed — and in his numerous conversations with ship's masters, Philip had never once heard anyone fault James. Edmund, in contrast, had had plenty of critics.

Because of the success of James' selfless and solitary mission, Philip had come to believe that James had, ultimately, been a greater man than Edmund. Of course, not everyone would have agreed with this private evaluation. Philip was well aware that a judgement of this kind depended on one's standard.

From childhood Edmund had occupied center stage —

49

first in the family, then in the town. He had invariably stolen the show. He had always been a great talker, and he had become used to being listened to and having his own way. Though increasingly lethargic physically, he had pushed forward opinions on every subject and he had chosen his words judiciously. He had become increasingly James' opposite.

Although James had never spared himself, Philip had observed that he had doled out words as carefully and reluctantly as some people parted with shillings. Yet, whatever the personal risk, James had always been ready to exert himself for others. So much so that by the age of 60 he had worn himself out. Although Philip had understood this, he had, in accepting the governorship of Sable Island, opted for the same sort of life as James.

* * *

James, Philip believed, had first met Henry Bayfield late in the summer of 1844. From the *Sylph* Philip had himself observed Bayfield's survey vessel, the *Gulnare*, in the vicinity of Scatarie, but, although their paths had crossed often in the next few years, he had not actually met the talented and dedicated chartmaker until several years later — in 1847, he thought. Then Bayfield had been surveying Port Hood Harbor and their meeting had been inevitable. At that time, as far as Philip could recall, they had spoken chiefly of James and Scatarie.

James and Bayfield had apparently hit it off at once. It had helped that they were of the same age and background. (James had gone to sea at 15, Bayfield at 11.) But what they had come together over — had seen eye to eye on — had been the errors both had perceived in the then current admiralty charts (DesBarres') of the approaches to Scatarie.

What had first alerted Bayfield to the problems mariners could face as they neared this island had been his own difficulties. Approaching from the south, he had been very much out in his reckonings. Despite clear weather and calm seas, the strength of the currents off Scatarie's east end had driven the *Gulnare* back to the east southeast some eighteen miles in eleven hours. For a while, not realizing what had been happening, Bayfield had searched for the light from James' lighthouse, but had seen no glimmer. It had been the all-encompassing darkness which had at length given him a clue to the idiosyncrasies of the currents — and his own consequent miscalculation.

Yet what had subsequently surprised Bayfield most about these currents had been the realization that one could not even count on being delayed by them. Under circumstances which varied only slightly from those he had first experienced — that is, on sailing northeastward across the same tract of water — he had perceived no current whatsoever.

But this was not all Bayfield had discovered when approaching Scatarie on other occasions. In taking soundings in the vicinity of the island over the next few years, it had become apparent to him that his findings had not jibed with DesBarres'. In the seventy-year-old admirality chart certain submerged rocks and ledges had not been marked. Small wonder indeed, he had observed, that masters navigating according to these faulty charts had run onto rocks where their way had been shown to be clear. The horrified and indignant Bayfield had been obliged to conclude that so many of the fatal shipwrecks recorded near this island need not have occurred.

Philip had been well aware that such findings had not been news to James — or, for that matter, to anyone in Sydney who had talked to Captain Dunbar or read the newspaper account of the wrecking of his ship, the *Sarah & Caroline*, in the autumn of 1840. At that time the master of this Boston vessel had been outspoken about laying the blame for the loss of his ship squarely on the faulty chart he had relied on . . . and James had backed him up.

In 1844, on their first meeting, Bayfield had told James that, in his opinion, establishing soundings for the vicinity of Scatarie was as important a priority as similar work which needed to be done off Sable Island. By 1848 — the year when several large vessels had foundered near Scatarie for the same apparent reason as the *Sarah & Caroline* — Bayfield had advised the admiralty to stop issuing charts for the Atlantic coast of Cape Breton.

With the 1850 publication of Bayfield's charts of Scatarie and Main-à-Dieu a new era in navigation along this

51

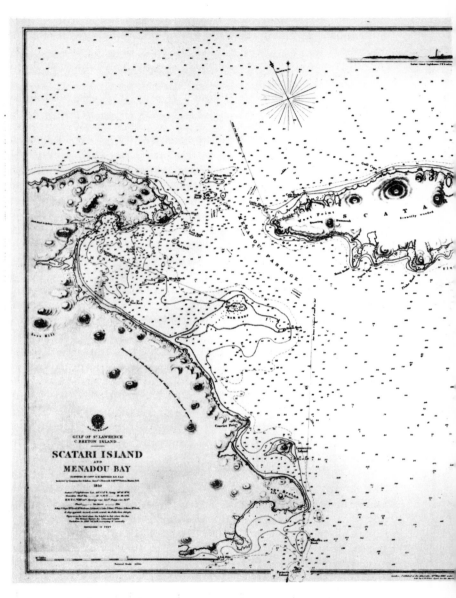

Chart of Scatarie (or Scatari) Island, Bayfield (1850)

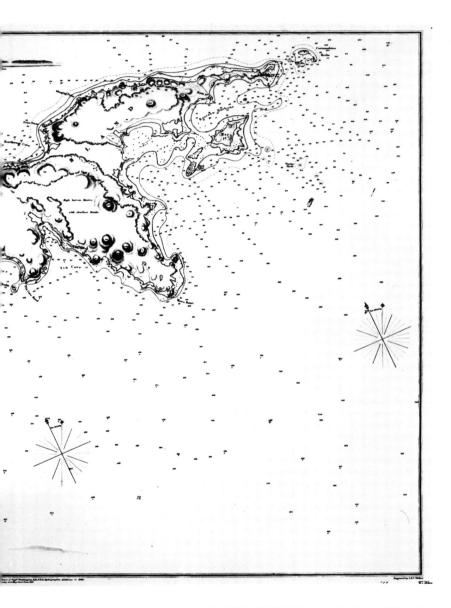

(B.A. Chart/no. 2730/1850 (1860) NMC 104395) National Archives of Canada

treacherous part of the Cape Breton coast began. Shipwrecks still occurred near Scatarie, but not with the same frequency as before. This island was no longer feared as it had once been. Consequently, by the early sixties, as Philip remembered well, Matthew McKenna, in his capacity as superintendent of lighthouses and humane establishments, had recommended cutting down on the number of men employed at Scatarie's lifesaving station. There were no longer prospects of the same number of wrecks or of a comparable amount of grisly and back-breaking labor which their predecessors of the previous decade had counted on.

* * *

Bayfield's chart had clearly depicted Scatarie Island in relation to the portion of the mainland with which it was most closely linked — namely, Main-à-Dieu. The association so apparent from a cartographical point of view was no less significant from a human one.

The inhabitants of Main-à-Dieu had long considered Scatarie an extension of their domain. It contributed significantly to their well-being. Not only did the island shield the village from many of the worst Atlantic gales, but it was an important source of livelihood. The villagers' fishing huts were there, and the vessels which were regularly wrecked on the island's shoals had, over the years, provided them with a good many of life's necessities and a few luxuries besides.

If James had not been accepted as one of the villagers, Philip doubted if he could have run the Scatarie Establishment. A superintendent on this island could, he felt certain, never manage without their support.

As it was, they had felt responsible for James. He and Catherine had lived amongst them. Their children had played with his. Catherine had died in the village . . . .

Moreover, the villagers had admired James. He had been an experienced seafaring man in a place which depended solely on the sea. And if he had had important connections in Sydney, that was fine too; so had several others. Among these were John Leonard, master of the vessel which later carried whale oil to Scatarie to fuel its light, and the masters of a

54

number of the vessels which regularly transported coal from the Sydney mines to the outside world.

For if the link between Scatarie Island and Main-à-Dieu was strong, the connection between Main-à-Dieu and Sydney was equally significant. For the inhabitants of Main-à-Dieu, Cape Breton still seemed a province separate from the rest of Nova Scotia, and Sydney its capital. It was from Sydney that mail and provisions, coal and customs officials were dispatched.

Halifax was too far away. Unless prodded by Edmund, Uniacke or Young, members of the House there seemed rarely to remember that Cape Breton had come under their jurisdiction. Only during real emergencies, like the shipping crises of the early thirties, had they briefly attended to their responsibilities here.

However, Philip could see now that, once the lighthouses and humane establishments on Scatarie and St. Paul's had been built and staffed, members of the Halifax House had turned their attention elsewhere. Less and less news of the disasters which continued to occur in the vicinities of these treacherous rocks seemed to have filtered through to House members. When it did, it seemed scarcely to register.

Philip recalled the time when lightkeeper Donald Moon had been drowned in a rescue attempt off St. Paul's. The House members had seemed unwilling to attend to the petition of his destitute wife and child. Only when John Campbell, superintendent of St. Paul's Establishment, had intervened, had the House reluctantly agreed to set aside £15 to prevent Ann Moon and her child from starving to death.

Gradually, as Edmund had noted, reports of shipwrecks off Scatarie and St. Paul's were no longer recorded in the House *Journal*. No wonder James had been increasingly lax about sending in details of Scatarie wrecks: no one in control seemed to read his reports. Only Jacob Miller had turned up once a year (for an hour and a half in midsummer) to check on the light and the Establishment — and then only when it was not too rough or foggy for the *Daring* to anchor off the east end of the island. For most Haligonians it had seemed as if the only Humane Establishment in the province was the one on Sable Island.

V

Sable Island 1855-1873
waning sand crescent

"The island is about thirty miles in length, very low, and
without a tree or other object to distinguish it from the
surrounding ocean which it so much resembles in color
under certain effects of light and shade that a ship might
run upon it almost before her seamen were aware of it."

— Captain Preble 1873 (condensed from the *London
Nautical Magazine and Naval Chronicle*, 1842).

* * *

"The ocean bounds him everywhere. Spread East and
West, he views the narrow Island in form of a bow, as if
the great Atlantic waves had beat it around, no where
much above a mile wide, twenty-six miles long
including the dry bars, and holding a shallow lake
thirteen miles long in its centre."

— J. Bernard Gilpin, B.A., M.D. MRSC., 1858

* * *

". . . a low-lying island in the Atlantic in lat. 44 N. and
long. 60 W., 85 miles east of Nova Scotia. It is a chain of
sand dunes enclosing a lagoon, and is such a menace to

57

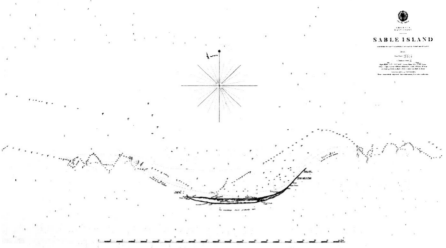

Chart of Sable Island, Bayfield 1853

(B.A. Chart/no. 2171/1853 NMC 103484) National Archives of Canada

Map of Sable Island, Bayfield, 1853

[Enlarged and labelled by Peter Mitcham] (B.A. Chart/no 2171/1853 NMC 103684)
National Archives of Canada

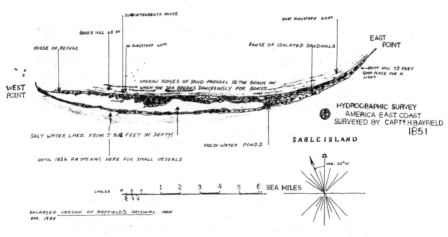

navigation that the government of Canada maintains two lighthouses there. It was formerly 40 miles long and is now but 20, gradually sinking . . . ."

— *The Encyclopedia Americana*, 1938.

Long before Philip had ever set foot on Sable, he had been well aware of the paradoxical nature of that island's reputation. This waning sand crescent, so much further out to sea than any of Nova Scotia's other offshore islands, had long since been invested with personality. It was said to be benevolent or malevolent, depending upon the experience and temperament of the narrator. As far as Philip could judge, this dual vision of the island's innate potential for good or evil had existed for hundreds of years. Few people, he gathered, had been able to hold a neutral view of this place.

There had, it seemed, always been the idealistic practical men — like Joe Howe and Dr. Gilpin in his own time — who had chosen to visit this island with an eye to assessing its usefulness. After tabulating the abundant and virtually untapped natural resources and advantages of the, to them, fascinating and even tranquil domain, they had concluded that the island could be made extraordinarily productive — an earthly paradise indeed.

And they had returned to Halifax to preach or write (or both) with almost evangelical fervor of their visions of this potential Eden. Philip himself had listened with interest to Joe Howe and reflected briefly on the satisfaction the person who could shape this man's dreams into reality would feel.

Like others in the early and mid-fifties, he had pondered Howe's and Gilpin's lengthy and convincing catalogues of the island's natural advantages: the abundant fresh water to be found either in the dune-protected lagoon or by digging down under the sand almost anywhere to a depth of about two feet; the cranberries which grew so prolifically that systematic harvesting could produce a crop sufficient to stave off scurvy aboard all his majesty's ships entering Halifax Harbor; the root vegetables — more than enough to feed the island population — which grew with surprising vigor in the sand after being fertilized with quantities of manure; the unique breed of wild horses, which, if properly selected and appropriately advertised for their strength and sturdiness, could be sold to greater advantage on the mainland than previously; the nutritious wild grasses, available year round to feed these creatures and domestic stock as well; the flocks of wildfowl which not only provided delicate fresh meat during the fall migration, but a winter's store besides; the barrels of oil from the flourishing colony of seals — enough to fuel lighthouses all along the coasts of Nova Scotia; the huge schools of cod and mackerel just off shore; the quantities of lobsters and crabs to be plucked from the shallows near the beach; the lumber, cloth, spirits, coal and other salvageable goods cast up upon the shores . . . .

But the men who returned home to inspire and entertain the elite of Halifax with such glowing accounts of Sable Island's potential had not been residents of this place. They did know what it was like to be responsible for coping with the emergencies, the boring daily chores, the confrontations, the correspondence with uncomprehending mainland officials . . . . Philip himself had learned the hard way what a difference residency on this island made to one's perspectives.

Howe and Gilpin had been privileged visitors. They had not been called on to risk their lives in the surf, year after year, nor had they been intimately involved in the tedious and troublesome aftermath of shipwrecks. They had not experienced the backbreaking round-the-clock labor of getting people and goods ashore before a ship broke up. They had not had to bury the dead; neither had they been obliged to clothe, shelter and feed hundreds of castaways for days . . . or weeks . . . or even months at a time, whilst praying hourly for a miracle of Biblical proportions to provide sufficient loaves and fishes. They had not known what was entailed in settling the disputes which inevitably arose when such disparate sorts of human beings were forced to live uncomfortably and at close quarters with people they would normally never associate with; . . . nor had they tried to separate a drunken crew of shipwrecked sailors from the barrels of rum and port which they had found cast up like themselves upon the shore . . . .

60

They had, moreover, never had to patrol the beaches during winter gales . . . and then return home to make polite conversation with a contentious ship's captain and a vicar's spoiled cousin, who, billeted indefinitely in the two best bedrooms, issued forth at regular intervals to complain about their cramped quarters, the limited choice of books in the "library" which Miss Dix had provided, and the lack of variety in the fare placed on the table at Main Station.

Eventually even Joe Howe, some years after his original and positive assertions about Sable, had done an about face. In a poem which had been briefly the rage in Halifax he had referred to the island as:

"Dark Isle of mourning! . . .
The Atlantic's charnel — desolate and drear . . ."

But by February 1858 when Howe's revised view was being delivered before the Athenaeum Society and quoted in Halifax drawing rooms, Philip had already spent more than two years patrolling the sands on which, according to Howe in his more somber mood,

"The broken waters by the winds are pressed, —
Roaring like fiends of hell which know no rest . . ."

arrival: September 1855

"... the crews here at present are the poorest I have had since I came to the island ..."

— M.D. McKenna, in a letter to the Chairman of the Board of Works, written on Sable Island, February 27, 1855

Philip had been told that autumn was a bad time to arrive on Sable Island. He had not guessed how bad. Anyway, he had had no choice: that was when he had been sent. McKenna, his predecessor, had left for Halifax on September 5.

His own voyage out had been fine enough. Susannah had found it a bit rough, but it had been nothing to upset a seafaring man like himself. He had in fact rather enjoyed it.

The *Daring* was somewhat the worse for wear, but a sturdy enough schooner for all that; and Daly was not only a first rate captain but a friend besides. They had had a chance to talk over old times, to reminisce about their days on the fisheries' patrols, to recall the shenanigans of certain delinquent American fishing captains.

As they had chatted in the wheelhouse, Philip had also had an opportunity to study Darby's 1823 chart of the island — the one Howe had found fault with in 1850 because he considered it outdated then. It was true that a lot of sand had shifted since Darby's drawing had been done. However, as Daly had pointed out, it was the captains who had navigated *without* Darby's chart and the warnings he had inscribed on it who had run aground on Sable Island. Philip himself had, he recalled, managed fine with it when he had taken the *Sylph* to Sable in the spring of '45. The new chart, though — the one from Bayfield's 1851 survey which Howe had insisted on — was, Daly had had to admit, an improvement.

Philip's interest in the charts had set Daly talking about Darby. Darby, Daly had remarked, had never been given his due ... well, not by his own government anyway ... particularly at the end of his superintendency. He had been dismissed because of a series of accusations which anyone in his right mind would have known were false. But then, Daly had added with a seaman's distaste for officialdom: "Who could make most of the Halifax bureaucrats understand the problems of life offshore?" After all, he had reminisced, hadn't both he and Philip had plenty of difficulties three years earlier trying to explain the nature of their confrontations with the American fishing captains?

Then, after a pause, Daly had returned to his original tack . . . . Darby's fate, he had observed, had seemed somewhat similar to McKenna's. Both men, he had noted, had received gold medals and citations for valor from foreign governments — and then, not long afterwards, been recalled to Halifax. It had, he had noted, taken years before the House had seen fit to grant Darby a small pension.

Daly had reckoned that both Darby and McKenna had been too able, increasingly too much in charge of affairs on the island, too loathe to listen to advice from Halifax, too full of recommendations about policy changes which would benefit the employees of the Establishment, too ready to demand a greater share of the salvage money for the employees and proper rewards for those who risked their lives in the surf to save crews of stranded or wrecked vessels.

McKenna especially, Daly had gone on, had been no slouch — although he had seemed very opinionated for such a young man. He had, for instance, just that year made no bones about telling anyone in authority that his crews were the poorest he'd had since his arrival on the island, and that he needed better men. Probably because of his complaints and outspokenness a number of the men had returned to Halifax on the *Daring* that April and May.

But then, Daly had pointed out, he'd had trouble that year with his own men on the *Daring*. He had found one of them asleep in his anchor watch, another pair who were lightfingered, and a steward who had attempted (twice) to jump overboard rather than make the crossing to Sable Island in mid-December. When Daly had restrained the latter, he had told Philip, the wretched man had tried to beat his brains out by banging his head repeatedly on the deck . . . .

Whether he had had the upper hand or not, McKenna had not been backward about coming forward, Daly had continued. Even when he knew he was being replaced — not until that very August, Daly had thought — McKenna had sent a letter off right away informing the members of the Board of Works that he was anxious to leave the island with his family before the bad weather set in . . . . The Board, Daly had noted, had listened, and he had taken the McKennas back to the mainland early that September. He had even remembered the exact date, the 5th — a sad day — the very day the year before that they had buried their infant son . . . .

"Now, there was a determined man if ever I saw one!" had been Daly's refrain. "I don't suppose they've heard the last of him yet in Halifax . . . ." And Daly had been right.

* * *

Daly had anchored well off the north side of Sable Island, and almost at once the men of the Establishment had put out for the *Daring* in one of the lifeboats.

The ride in through the surf that first time had been enough to take anyone's breath away. Philip had never before been borne in so fast or perched so precariously on the crest of a wave. He felt as he imagined the voyageurs must have felt shooting the rapids of some colossal torrent — though more vulnerable, he guessed, since he was without their experience and training. One false move, he knew, could catapult them all into the water, and there were no guarantees that if this happened they would ever resurface.

Despite the risks, or perhaps because of them, the men had moved through their routines with perfect poise, strokes synchronized, limbs attuned, as if some unseen telegraph cable had connected them and kept them constantly informed of the others' movements. When the boat had been thrown up on the beach, the crew had moved again as one, jumping out and heaving the boat forward just in time to escape the reach of the next wave and its undertow.

The passengers had not even got wet. Someone, McKenna, he supposed, had done a wonderful job of training this crew; and afterwards it seemed likely that the constant dangers and difficulties of the situation had kept them on their toes.

But although he had congratulated the men on their

expert handling of the small boat, Philip had thought at once that they had not been pleasantly responsive. Surly had been the word most descriptive of their attitude. And, as he had been shown the Establishment and escorted up the tower, his impression of a general reluctance to accept his presence had grown. These people had been civil — but only just.

He had not understood what the matter was, either then or later . . . though eventually he had, in the light of subsequent events, laid the blame on McKenna. That the men were still loyal to McKenna seemed obvious.

McKenna had been recalled. They did not want his replacement. It had seemed as simple and clear-cut as that.

Philip guessed that they would have treated any new superintendent as they had treated him, but this impression had not eased the situation. The mood on the island had been ugly. It was as if some sort of evil essence was being continually released from these inhospitable sands.

And, despite his usually cheerful disposition, Philip had felt the poison entering his system. He had been increasingly tense, increasingly suspicious and apprehensive. The situation had been depressing in the extreme. There had seemed no solution. What could he do or say to bring these stolid and unsmiling people over to his side?

However, if they insisted on being hateful, he had vowed privately, he would reciprocate . . . and this dreadful situation, this most inauspicious of beginnings, he had surmised, had been McKenna's doing.

McKenna

"... beware of him (McKenna), and fear him most when he smiles most for he is certain to betray ...."

— in a letter from Philip Dodd to Hugh Bell, Board of Works, written September 19, 1856.

In sorting out his papers Philip had come upon jottings for a letter. The statement which had stood out from the spidery words scrawled across the now yellowed page was this one. If the strange fragment had not been in his own handwriting, he would now never have quite believed that the circumstances had been desperate enough to have elicited so disturbed a response.

No wonder Bell had not known how to react! The tone of the letter must scarcely have seemed to him that of a former ship's captain, a fisheries boarding officer of long standing, a newly-appointed superintendent of the world's most important Humane Establishment, a man long used to making disciplined and formal entries in official logs and journals. It sounded instead, Philip now had to admit, more like the ravings of some half-crazed player in a cheap melodrama, giving the sort of self-indulgent and unbelievable performance he himself would ordinarily never have countenanced.

Yet, as he thought back to the days immediately after his arrival on Sable Island and reviewed the events which had followed the confrontation with McIsaac, some of the old unsettling emotions returned. They were not so strong, but they were still there. Time and his subsequent knowledge of McKenna's own exasperations and outbursts had only partly altered his perspectives. A certain puzzlement remained.

* * *

The undercurrents of unrest which Philip had felt so strongly as soon as he set foot on the island had soon surfaced. He had indeed expected trouble — a questioning of his authority, perhaps a direct confrontation. Yet when it had happened he had been caught off guard.

The men had been duck hunting that day, and, as was

usual on the island every autumn, they had shot great numbers of black ducks. Morale was better than it had been since his arrival. Everyone had seemed pleased with the hunters' success. The birds provided a most welcome change of fare.

The hunters, though clearly satisfied with their day's work, were cold and tired and wet. They had cleaned their birds, but not plucked them. Their hands, they said, were too numb — and, subsequently, too hot and swollen to do the job. Philip had not insisted. He could see that they had had enough. Instead, he had told McIsaac, who had not gone hunting, to pluck the birds.

McIsaac had refused. He would, he had said, not do the job alone: he would only pluck the birds if the others helped him . . . or, if they couldn't do that, at least if they were employed at something else. It was unfair, he claimed, if he had to work all evening by himself while the others relaxed.

There had been a hush in the mess room following McIsaac's outburst. Most of the men had not heard all the argument. Only Gaspar Graham,* the foreman, had been standing close enough for every word to register. Nevertheless, the men were silent and motionless. There was a feeling of trouble in the air. Mrs. McIsaac had stopped where she was, halfway between the stove and the table, the steaming pot extended.

Philip knew and the men knew that this was mutinous behaviour, not to be tolerated on an island outpost any more than it would have been on shipboard. Philip's mind had raced back over the miserable days since his arrival, the rebelliousness he had felt in the men, and he knew that he had to take a firm hand now or lose his grip on the situation forever.

"You're through, then . . . through, McIsaac," he had announced. "You're to go ashore on the *Daring* on her next trip."

McIsaac, sullen and stolid, had left the room. Mrs. McIsaac had retreated to the stove with the pot still extended

---

* Graham and his family left the island about a year later (on October 23, on the *Daring*). He had not worked out as foreman and Philip had had to demote him.

and had stood there with her back to the rest of the room. The men had begun to talk quietly. Philip had gone into the sitting room. He regretted not having been able to handle McIsaac's mutiny as he would have on shipboard.

Yet for a while the air seemed to have cleared. McIsaac had been sent back to Halifax, Mrs. McIsaac had been allowed to stay on as cook until summer — and he had put in for a man to replace her then — and the men had set about their tasks more willingly, he had thought.

But McIsaac's return to the mainland had not put an end to the affair. No sooner, it seemed, had he arrived in Halifax than he had contacted McKenna, who was by then working for the Department of Public Works — supervising, of all things, humane establishments and lighthouses. McIsaac had told McKenna about his dismissal, claiming he had been unfairly treated. And the unthinkable had happened. McKenna had taken McIsaac's part.

For a while the matter had rested. Or perhaps it had simply been that no word of it had got out to the island. McIsaac had been to see McKenna in early December, and the rest of the winter had been so harsh that communications between Halifax and Sable Island had been halted for months.

Then in July McKenna had been sent back to the island to investigate the workings of the Establishment. What a nightmare it had been! . . . McKenna had been calm and civil and smiling. Heaven only knew what had been going on beneath that even surface! The men had once more rallied around him, or so it had seemed . . . . Mrs. McIsaac had apparently added her complaints to her husband's, and Philip had assumed that some of the other women had supported her.

Part of this new hostility had been, Philip surmised, the result of his outspokenness about wishing to ban the men's wives and children from the island, together with his determination to acquire a male cook at Main Station. The situation had become increasingly insupportable. His second year on the island was about to begin, and yet day after day had passed without his having had any word of how he stood with the authorities in Halifax.

It was then, in mid-September, in the most agitated of states that he had written Bell, wondering what McKenna had

68

told him — and warning him that McKenna's viewpoint was unreliable, that he was two-faced. It had been unfortunate, Philip could see more clearly than ever now, that he had sounded so unreliable himself — so much like a lunatic in fact, while McKenna had kept cool and smiling.

* * *

And then, gradually, the turmoil had subsided. The unrest had abated — apparently of its own accord — in the same way a gale off the island blew itself out. Winter had come again. After December no vessels had gone aground. Neither the *Daring* nor the *Wave* had appeared for months. The island community had been left to regulate itself.

Philip had worked the men and himself hard. That had been part of the cure; that together with the building, which had given all of them a sense of worth and pride in their accomplishments.

And then one bright, calm day toward spring when he had taken one of the men out fishing, Philip had heard a story which put McKenna in a new light. The man, who had been on the island several years before when the incident occurred, had told him an odd tale about McKenna losing his temper — going right off the deep end indeed — over the refusal of a man called Brady to obey him.

Philip still recalled the gist of the man's story.

He had told how three years previously, in mid-May, some of the men had been salvaging from one of the wrecks. McKenna, as usual, had been directing them. They had been — all except Brady the carpenter — at a considerable distance from McKenna, the team and the wagon, when one man, looking back, had seen the team bolt in McKenna's direction. McKenna had apparently gesticulated and jumped aside. Brady, who had been near the team, had not moved. The horses had veered off, just missing McKenna, and the next moment McKenna had been on Brady, kicking and pummelling him to within an inch of his life.

By the time the men had come up, the scuffle was over. McKenna was standing over Brady, who, bloody and winded, lay on the sand. The teamster had hurried off after the runaway horses, but the other men had stood by, transfixed by

McKenna's explosion, taking in with apparent difficulty the vituperative words directed down at the almost unconscious Brady: "You insolent bastard! You're finished! . . . I told you to stop that team and you just stood there with that silly smirk on your face. You bloody fool! I could have been killed!"

Then he had turned on the gaping crew: "And let no man amongst you ever mistake me! When I give an order I expect to be obeyed! At once!"

The men, Philip's fishing companion had told him, had never seen McKenna riled like that before — or, indeed, ever again.

McKenna, he had remarked, had sent Brady back to Halifax a few days later on the *Daring*, together with, everyone had surmised, a letter of explanation to Hugh Bell.

* * *

The fisherman's story had helped Philip come to terms with his own situation, and given him hope too that everything might blow over. McKenna, then, had faced the same stupid sort of insubordination from Brady that he had from McIsaac — and McKenna had reacted more violently than Philip himself. How then, Philip had wondered, could McKenna ever have dared to judge him? He had been more puzzled than ever about McKenna's stance.

Now, however, he thought he understood Hugh Bell's lack of action. Bell must have remembered McKenna's difficulties with Brady and thought that Philip's problems with McIsaac fit the pattern of Sable Island confrontations. Bell had perhaps assumed that there must be something provocative in the very air of the place that caused hitherto sane and sensible men to lose their balance over trivial occurrences.

Philip had never known Bell's exact feelings. Perhaps Bell had not given the matter much thought at all. After all, Sable Island had not been the only island outpost where there had been problems to settle.

Whatever had transpired behind closed doors in Halifax, by the next summer — 1857, Philip's second summer on Sable Island — a new superintendent of the Board of

Works, William Condon, had come out to inspect the Humane Establishment. Satisfied with the way the island was being governed, Condon had reported favorably on the amount and quality of the building which had been done and on the harmonious accord he had observed between Philip and his men.

And as the years had gone by and the whole matter of McKenna's apparent antipathy to himself and his way of governing the island had receded into the past, Philip had even begun to feel sorry for McKenna. McKenna, he guessed, had been hard-pressed to understand why he had been dispossessed. He had probably assumed — and not without reason — that Philip had got his position as Governor of Sable Island through influential connections.

After all the years of building, all the planning, all the sacrifices, dangers and difficulties, it was not surprising that McKenna had resented being uprooted. Philip could see now that it did not seem fair . . . . probably had not been fair.

McKenna, he had had to admit at last, was a very able man — a first rate lifesaver and salvager, an exemplary superintendent and builder. And if he had lost his temper on one occasion and been caught up in uncontrollable jealousy on another, well, no man is perfect . . . .

builders

"... a foolish man ... built his house upon the sand: And the rain descended, and the floods came, and the winds blew, and beat upon that house; and it fell: and great was the fall of it."

St. Matthew 7:26, 27

Sable Island had always been better for wreckers than builders. Even without visiting this extended sandbar, its long-established name — *Sable*, the French word for sand — would have indicated to the thoughtful person that this must be so.

Philip himself had been dead set against building on sand. His earliest recollections from countless Sunday services at St. George's had conditioned him not even to entertain the notion. The Biblical injunction to build on rock, not sand, had long since settled into his subconscious. Besides, what Cape Bretoner, born and bred in such a dominantly rocky natural environment, would have considered building on sand? If he had, he would have been almost as hard-pressed to find a sufficient stretch of it along the Atlantic coast as his predecessors at Canso or Halifax.

That the Biblical injunction made good sense had been proved time and time again on this island. Apart from McKenna's recent buildings which, Philip had had to admit, continued to stand firm, most of the houses, barns and sheds from his other predecessors' reigns stood on splayed beams, had collapsed, been buried by the shifting sands, or been carried away as readily as children's beach castles when powerful tides and currents ate into the land.

The buildings which had been most vulnerable to the sea had been those on the west end. There, the land had been gobbled up at an alarming rate. Small wonder that some years prior to going to Sable — early in Darby's time, he thought — the principal station had been moved from this end to the middle of the island.

In his own time and McKenna's the erosion has slowed a good deal due, apparently, to the formation of a new series of sandbars just offshore. The waves now broke first upon these. But how long they would stay in place was anybody's guess.

Anyway, whatever the warnings, evangelical or commonsensical, the Sable Island builder clearly had no choice of foundation. Sand was all there was. The granite, on which the sand was reputed to have lodged thousands of years before, was, if it existed, too far down to be of any use. Besides, anyone who attempted to reach this rock would soon be deterred by coming upon water — first fresh, then salt.

On his arrival Philip had intended to set about building at once. Whatever the drawbacks of this place, he had determined to do his best to make it into the sort of permanent and thriving colony Howe had envisioned after his visit five years earlier. McKenna had built well, despite the sand. He, Philip, would build better.

However, at first these dreams had seemed impossible to fulfil. McKenna had completed so many projects, especially in his last few years on the island, that, at first glance, there seemed nothing left to build — except an oilhouse at the principal station and a boathouse near the landing on the north shore. But each of these required only a few days of concerted effort and presented no particular difficulty or challenge.

Philip's seaman's eye had taken immediate note of these small matters, while completely overlooking the importance and pressing need for a new barn at the principal station. In retrospect he could only attribute this oversight to his absolute lack of agricultural experience: he had never up until his arrival on Sable thought about livestock or crops except in so far as they were necessary for provisioning a ship or a store. Now, all at once, on this island he had had to consider field and animal husbandry. Crucial to the latter was the way the stock was housed.

That construction of this barn was to provide the foundation of his own confidence about overseeing the building of several major and significant structures on Sable Island the better part of two decades later was an irony he had not been able to appreciate until recently. At the time he had been too busy with the day to day business of the Establishment to be concerned with future perspectives.

The start had been slow and inauspicious. Just to get a crew on the job had taken more than a year. This had been due partly to the way the men had balked at taking orders from him at first, but mostly the problem had been the wrecks. It was understood that the role of wrecker-salvager of whatever could be saved from the vessels which went aground — took precedence over that of builder. And, for more than a year after his arrival, coping with the wrecks, together with just maintaining the daily routines, had used up the time and energy of all hands.

Philip had wanted to begin the barn in August 1856, or at least some time during that first summer on the island, but this had been impossible. From early June there had been scarcely a moment to spare — not even time to put up the oilhouse or boathouse. Preparing the soil for cabbages, turnips, potatoes; mowing and bringing in the successive crops of hay — first the cultivated, then the wild; catching the wild horses — some twenty of them to send off on the *Daring* for sale on the mainland, and several to break in for the Establishment; killing and salting down the winter's pork and beef; sawing and splitting wood from former wrecks on the south beach and then boating it across the lake; planting, weeding, digging up and storing the root vegetables; picking and later culling cranberries; cooping barrels . . . All these tasks had taken more time than he had reckoned on.

But it had been the wrecks that summer and fall which had really made building out of the question. No sooner, it seemed, had one been attended to, its crew and cargo recovered and dispatched to Halifax on the *Daring* or the *Wave*, than another was on the shoals. Then the whole exhausting and time-consuming process had begun all over again. Like the farming, wrecking had proved to be another pursuit whose difficulties he would never formerly have guessed at.

Three stranded vessels between the beginning of July and early December had meant that there had been no opportunity to start building. On only two or three occasions during these frantically busy months had he got the men to haul timbers for the new barn, but it had been mid-January before he had been able to assign George Walker and two other men the job of framing the structure. From then until May, when everyone had given a hand with the shingling, these three had labored. Philip had watched them framing in the teeth of February gales while three or four other men had dug and

74

wheeled away sand (and sometimes snow), levelled the site, and laid the sills.

Philip had kept Walker and his helpers on the framing because he suspected the others didn't have the know-how. Anyway, he needed the rest to haul timbers. Day after day he had sent them off to Seal Cove with the teams. And once in early February he had even had all hands rafting timbers from the cove to Main Station. A chill and miserable task that had been!

Still, despite the weather, the building had taken shape. And month after month not a single vessel had run ashore. The men had even been in good spirits — that was, until the death of Peter de Young's child early in March.

Peter was, Philip had thought from the first, the ablest of his men — the one he had decided to choose as foreman of the lifeboat crew. The others liked him and looked up to him.

In such a closely-knit community the death of any child sent a chill through everyone's heart. It might be their own dear boy or girl next. And on this island there was no resident doctor to keep death at bay.

Philip had known that the island men and their wives thought that he and Susannah did not really understand — that they were too old, too aloof, too privileged to comprehend the agony of losing a child. How were they to know about young Philip's death? Neither he nor Susannah ever spoke of it now, even to each other . . . And how to tell the men and their wives that living on the mainland with a doctor in hailing distance did not guarantee the health and survival of one's offspring? . . . Trying to explain these things was hopeless . . . They had not even tried.

Still, this tragic incident had confirmed Philip's original impression that the men's dependents should not be allowed on the island. The Sable Island Establishment, he had thought, should be run like a ship. Those who signed up for duty — except perhaps the 'captain' — would have to leave their wives and children behind on the mainland.

There had been too many accidents and near accidents in the past to fault this stand, Philip had reckoned. Why even McKenna's wife and twins had just missed being drowned in the surf on their return from Halifax. And who knew whether his wife and that fifth baby would have survived at all if McKenna had not used all his wiles to keep Dr. Gilpin on the island until after the delivery.

Yet as the years had passed Philip had seen that, reasonable though his viewpoint had seemed at first, it had not been realistic. The establishment would never be staffed if the men were not allowed to bring their families with them.

The comfort their wives and children provided was, he could see now, about all the satisfaction the men had got, apart from a bare living, from their years of hard labor on Sable Island. After all their slavery — yes, that was undoubtedly the correct word — they had no land to call their own, nothing built with their hands that they could say was theirs, nothing to turn to in their old age, nothing to show their grandchildren . . . As soon as their youth and vigor were spent, they were put aboard the *Daring* or its successors and shipped back to the mainland.

But Philip had only really understood their fate when he had realized that it differed very little from his own, Hodgson's, Darby's, and Alexander Cocken's (on McNutt's Island) . . . and James' . . .; indeed, from that of nearly all those island keepers who had guarded remote island outposts along Nova Scotia's coasts with care, courage and integrity and then been abandoned in their old age and infirmity — cast up like driftwood from a wreck. The office-bound bureaucrats who had presided without either understanding or appreciation over their life's work had refused them pensions or compensation in their declining years . . . or had haggled over a few pounds until the would-be recipients were heartsick and disillusioned.

Only McKenna of all those he knew had got ashore unscathed, his youthful vigor still intact . . . . And then he had joined the bureaucrats.

Philip guessed that it would always be the same. There could never be any firm meeting ground for men whose lives had been spent in such different worlds.

How, for instance, could the chairman and members of the Board of Public Works ever hope to understand the workings of the Sable Island Establishment when their inspections were years apart and then only for a day or two in midsummer? Philip particularly recalled their first visit during the third summer of his tenure. The *Daring* had arrived on the last day of June. The chairman and his Board had come ashore, toured the island the following day, and sailed back to Halifax on the second of July.

* * *

But to get back to the builders . . .

For the successful building, Philip recalled, there had not been another such year during his entire Sable Island rule as that second year — 1857 . . . that is, until his final few years.

In 1857 there had not been a single wreck. So after the completion of the barn, he had got the men going on the boathouse and then the oilhouse. The boathouse, it was true, had scarcely been used that year; but the oilhouse — once the hearth and chimney had been completed with bricks brought up from the foot of the lake — had been in almost constant use. The men had been kept busy for months hunting seals and cutting up the fat. He had, he remembered, taken part in a good many of these sealing excursions himself.

Yet the building had continued — a wagon for salvaging, barrels by the hundreds, a smoke house, fences . . . .

But these had not been the grandiose projects Philip had once dreamed of. It was not until years later, in 1871, that his chance had come to preside over the sort of structure he had first thought of building on Sable Island. The government had at last given the go-ahead for two lighthouses — one to be constructed on either end of the island.

Long before coming to Sable Island, Philip had heard about the controversies over whether or not to erect a lighthouse, or lighthouses, on this dangerous sandsprit. Sea captains, merchants and politicians had, he knew, argued the pros and cons ever since the turn of the century at least — certainly ever since the founding of the Humane Establishment. Later Edmund had told him of the squabbles in the House on this subject, and his old friend, James Daly of the *Daring* had also broached the subject to him on several occasions.

McKenna, like Superintendent Darby before him, had

77

turned thumbs down on the idea. Lighthouses, he had said, would do no good on Sable Island. But Howe had said they would, and Philip had agreed with him.

Here had been his chance. He would supervise the construction of two lighthouses — one at the east end first, and then another even taller, grander structure at the west end.

These, he had thought, would be permanent and significant accomplishments to leave behind. And, despite the passing of time, and the mellowing of his feelings of hostility towards McKenna, he still could not help thinking secretly that McKenna, for once, had not been so smart in refusing such a challenge. He, Philip, would now have the credit.

And yet, relatively early on in his superintendency, there had been one significant warning sign at least that the building of lighthouses on this waning sand crescent — particularly one close to the west end — would be a precarious and probably unwise venture. It was just that, at the time, he had been unwilling to consider the long-term implications of what he had seen.

At the beginning of 1858 — in February or March — Daly had petitioned the House for light stations on Sable Island. Philip and a good many others had supported him. As captain of the Establishment's vessel — the man who visited Sable most regularly and at all seasons of the year — Daly, it seemed, had the right to speak out and be listened to if anyone had.

And then, that very spring, there had been an ominous incident — portentious even. Or had he read the signs aright? The west end house of refuge had been inundated by the sea from the north. It had needed to be replaced at once, but in a new location closer to Main Station.

Philip had been worried enough at the time to have written Thorne, then Chairman of the Board of Works, asking him to come out to the island as soon as the weather improved. Philip had wanted him to see for himself, had wanted him to assess the damage and make recommendations . . . .

But then, after the house of refuge had been rebuilt, Philip had been caught up once more in the busy everyday routines. He had filed his memories and fears about the eroding west end at the back of his mind. He had begun, once

West End House of Refuge (Sable Island)
Dr. Gilpin, 1854. Admiral Digby Library and Historical Society

more, to look forward to the time when the construction of the lighthouses would begin. Besides, he had not been sure — was still not sure — about whether the undermining of the west end would continue. It was hard for anyone to predict how the winds and currents would finally shape this island.

* * *

It had all along been a question of money — or so Philip had thought. Building and maintaining lighthouses on Sable Island was going to cost too much. Even with infusions from the treasuries of the other provinces who would benefit from such lights — under sharing agreements like those long since arranged for the financing of Scatarie, Saint Paul's and Seal

Island stations — the main burden would still fall on Nova Scotia.

Besides, once McKenna had been installed in the board of Works office and Jacob Miller, his predecessor, ousted, there had been no powerful internal agitator (except Joe Howe, who had by then too many other matters on his mind) to stir up the Halifax establishment. Miller had pushed for lights on Sable Island for years. (James and Edmund and Daly had told Philip this.) Miller had even become so agitated about the question that he had written a report as far back as 1849 calling for portable lighthouses — ones which could be hauled to safer and more suitable locations as the sands shifted. He had criticized the government, accused it of apathy and indifference, even blamed it for several recent shipwrecks.

In view of such seemingly justifiable accusations, Daly had told Philip that he had never been able to fathom McKenna's stand against lighthouses on Sable — particularly as McKenna had sometimes during his last years on the island lit beacons when he had been expecting the *Daring*. On these occasions, Daly had, he said, congratulated McKenna for his foresight and told him that his light was often visible four miles out to sea. It had indeed, Philip assumed, been the very usefulness of this small and temporary guiding light which had prompted Daly's petition for a fixed and permanent beacon.

In any case, as far as Philip knew, it had only been after McKenna's return to Shelburne and the federal government's takeover of the Establishment after Confederation that the question of lighthouses on Sable Island had been seriously reconsidered. And by the early seventies it had been apparent that the prospective light stations had been designed not only to be permanent but also taller and stronger than others on the coast. Their broad bases were to be firmly planted in the sand and they were to cost, together, $80,000.

This had meant building on a scale never before envisaged for Sable Island. Consequently, Philip had in the end watched from the sidelines while the magnificent structures had gone up.

wreckers

"The establishment of Sable Island is now under the superintendance of Mr. P.S. Dodd, who was placed in charge 31st August, 1855 . . . .

As a stimulus to ascertain in case of wrecks, a percentage on property saved has always been allowed to the superintendant, and also a small sum to each of the men employed at any wreck. The percentage was formerly $1\frac{1}{2}$, but has from a short time previous to the late superintendant (McKenna) leaving, been $2\frac{1}{2}$ percent. But the auctioneers' commission, which used to be 5 percent, is reduced to $2\frac{1}{2}$, so that the owners of property are not injured, but rather benefited by the change. As to all other work on the Island I consider it a part of the ordinary duty, for which both superintendant and men are paid and supported, and for which no extra claim should be made. The bounty, in case of wrecks, is given as a stimulus to effort to save life and property."

— *Journal and Proceedings of the House of Assembly of Nova Scotia* (Appendix 13, 1856)

There was money to be made from the wrecks, and very little to be gained from building on the sands.

Because of the hoped-for profits from salvaging the wrecks, the early wreckers had camped out upon the sands long before the Humane Establishment had been set up. They had not bothered to build proper houses or plant gardens. They did not plan to stay. Desperate and violent men, who, it was said, would stop at nothing — including murder — to line their pockets, they counted on quick returns from their dangerous and uncomfortable sojourn on the bleak and treacherous sandbar.

Yet Philip could understand from his own experiences how terribly disappointed with their finds these men must often have been. He could almost sympathize with them. They must have risked their lives time after time — just as he and his men had — getting out to a wreck, only to find a cargo not worth salvaging: hundreds of barrels of damp flour; dried cod, sea-soaked; salt from the Turks, awash in salt water; limes and lemons from sunnier climes, on the verge of perishing.... And if, perchance, they found human beings aboard too, what were they to do with them? The wreckers had insufficient food and shelter for themselves.

Small wonder that after such frustrations and tragic confrontations some of them turned for comfort to a keg of rum or whisky salvaged from other wrecks; and, having drunk themselves into a stupor, froze to death upon the beach.

For salvaging was generally best in the worst weather. It was most often the winter gales which landed the wrecks upon the sands, and wreckers could not afford to wait for good weather to begin their work: the wreck might have been swept away by then.

Philip could well imagine the agony those early wreckers must have endured — working all day in the cold, soaked through, with no snug house, no hot meal to return to. Even with hearty fare and tightly constructed dwellings to come back to, he and his men had often been at the breaking point. No amount of booty, he reckoned, could have been worth the lifestyle of these former adventurers. But, of course, they had been driven by half-crazed visions of incredible riches — not, he thought, so unlike those of their more recent counterparts of '49 who had abandoned home and family to head for the gold fields of California. Perhaps, like the gold miners, some of Sable Island's turn-of-the-century wreckers had even achieved their goals . . . but at what cost!

The old time wreckers, Philip felt sure, would have been fed up with the cargoes of the vessels which had foundered on the island during the early years of his superintendency. No gold or silver, no gems or silks, no rich perfumes or exotic ornaments had come ashore during this time. Why for more than a year — all of 1857 and part of 1858 — there had been no wrecks at all! After a series of years like his own first three on Sable Island, the early wreckers — those who had salvaged before the days of the Humane Establishment — would undoubtedly have given up and returned to the mainland where almost any prospect would have seemed better.

Twenty-five hundred boxes of lemons all at once,

Wreckers' Den near Pond on the Isle of Sable
DesBarres. (PAC Neptune/vol. 2Pt. 6N080½ NMC 28177)
National Archives of Canada

hundreds of barrels of flour, fish, salt pork and beef — perishable goods all, and in quantities to boggle the mind! To be useful, such foodstuffs had to be retrieved carefully, stored in tight, dry places and delivered promptly to markets which could dispose of them at once. Without a large crew, without excellent lifeboats like the *Victoria,* without sizeable schooners like the *Daring*, the *Wave* and the *Crimea* standing by, without an eager mainland auctioneer, salvaging and disposing profitably of such provisions would have been impossible.

Philip had to admit that in general the salvage operations he had presided over had not only been easier than the early wreckers', but easier and more lucrative too than those of his more recent predecessors, the four superintendents who had come before him. Morris and Hodgson had counted themselves fortunate if they saw the supply boat twice a year. If there were wrecks between these appearances, they mostly had had to figure out a way to put up the rescued human beings and salvaged property as best they could — sometimes for months at a time. There were bound to be losses.

Even during Darby's tenure this situation had not improved greatly. It had been during McKenna's time that conditions had grown noticeably better. He had insisted that they had to improve. The *Daring*, for instance, had increased the number of yearly round trips between Halifax and Sable Island.

Then, from the beginning of his own superintendency, Philip realized, there had been a really dramatic improvement in the *Daring's* service. The perseverance of his friend Daly clearly had had much to do with this. But even Daly had been unable to make the last trip of the season, the December one, on a good many occasions. The weather had been altogether too wild.

Yet when there had been a lot of cargo to take off the island, the *Daring* — and sometimes several additional schooners — had plied regularly between Halifax and the island from early spring till late fall. Sometimes, Philip recalled, the *Daring* hove into sight twice in a three-week period: when, for instance, there had been all those boxes of lemons from the *Commerce*, and again the hundreds of barrels of flour from the *Alma*.

The *Daring* had best lived up to her name, however, when she had turned up from time to time during the worst winter months. With these more frequent and venturesome appearances, the Establishment had no longer seemed so isolated, so cut off.

The new lifeboats had made a great difference too. Arriving a couple of years before Philip himself, thanks to the combined efforts of Miss Dix and McKenna, they had proved so much more seaworthy than the old boats — though some of these had continued in service throughout the fifties.

Philip could not help wishing that James had had a lifeboat like the *Victoria* on Scatarie instead of the cumbersome and leaky dory he had made do with. Why, James' lifeboat had not been much better than the *Kitten*, the rowboat John had kept on the river at home for picnic excursions on fine summers' days! Still James had been a contemporary of Darby and life at all the Humane Establishments had been harder then.

Perhaps the greatest boost to morale on Sable Island had been the increase in the percentage — from $1\frac{1}{2}$ to $2\frac{1}{2}$ — which the men had received as a personal share from salvaging

Wrecking
Dr. Gilpin, 1854

a wreck. McKenna had won this increase in the month or two before his departure — and doubtless this had been one of the reasons the men had been so reluctant to see him replaced.

Still, despite such improvements, Philip had found that not a single one of the salvage operations had been what he would previously have described as a simple undertaking. For one thing, each one took far more time than he ever would have imagined possible before coming to Sable Island.

* * *

Despite the improved working conditions in his own time, Philip had found that salvaging even such relatively uncomplicated wrecks as the *Commerce* and the *Alma* had meant days of backbreaking dawn-till-dusk labor. After getting the crew off, the men had needed to spend roughly three weeks on each wreck. Just shifting the bulk of the cargo ashore and reloading it into the *Daring* and the *Wave* had taken that much time.   Afterwards there had been the sails, chains, hawsers and anchors to strip off.

But not every cargo could be transferred quickly and in its entirety to a conveniently waiting government schooner. Salvaging both the *Commerce* and the *Alma*, Philip recalled, had been complicated by the fact that these vessels had gone aground on the island's south shore.

For a good many days after the *Alma* had foundered, the *Daring* had not been able to get in close enough — a problem on the south side at the best of times. With the wind northwest and too much sea, she had had to stand off the island, and even when sea and wind had subsided and were blowing soft and southerly, the *Daring* had taken on a disappointingly small portion of the *Alma*'s flour, tea, tobacco, salt pork and beef.

The rest had had to be got in out of the weather — and so had begun the laborious hauling of boxes and barrels over the sand to the lake, boating everything across it, then hauling the goods up to the principal station with the teams.   Four loadings and unloadings!   A wonder only one of the men had been laid up with a bad back!

Much of the flour had had to be stored at the main station for months while the cooper had made new barrels. A good six months, Philip reckoned, had passed before they'd seen the last of the contents of the *Alma*'s hold.

Nearly every wreck had presented a different problem, Philip had found to his surprise.   Each had called for different strategies than the preceding one.   He had found himself coming up with surprising innovations — or utilizing those which the men recalled using on former wrecks. McKenna, he supposed, had thought up some of these.

One of the oddest innovations Philip had used on the *Alma* after all the visible cargo had been gotten off. Her captain had insisted that the bulk of the cargo consisted of barrels of salt meat in the hold. These Philip and his men had not been able to reach during the first three weeks of salvaging, since the contents of that part of the hold was under water.

They had tackled the problem on a fine mid-October day. The wind had been southwest, the sea moderate. Philip and two of the men had lowered the Establishment's small boat

Salvaging the *Alma*
Peter Mitcham

into the hold and then climbed down after it. There they had
sat with grappling hooks, fishing up barrels of pork and beef.
Even at the time Philip had seen in his mind's eye what a
ridiculous picture they made. It was hardly the situation an ex-
fisheries' officer or the Governor of Sable Island would have
expected to find himself in.   Philip had felt relieved that
Edmund and other members of Sydney's elite had not been
standing on the slanting deck of the *Alma* looking down into
the murky hold.   He had imagined the comical quips they
would have made.

Yet for every somewhat amusing interlude of this sort
— the kind which Philip had enjoyed retelling and even

embellishing for the entertainment of Elley and other light-hearted visitors — were their tragic counterparts. These he had tried — often unsuccessfully — to forget.

One unhappy incident which had continued to haunt him had occurred during his fourth autumn on Sable Island. It had stayed with him, he thought, because all the facts had never come to light.

He had only been able to guess the fate of the brig they had glimpsed too close to the northwest bar in that late October gale. She had apparently gone down in the same storm which had wrecked the brig *Lark* on the island's north side the following day.

He would never have known of the strange brig's tragic fate had his men not, by chance, found proof of an unidentified wreck thrown up upon the shore.

Philip had taken the men and a team onto the north beach to salvage the *Lark* which had been breaking up fast. However, it had been at once apparent that there was too much sea to work on the wreck.

So he had got all the men, except the two making the rounds, to collect and saw drift lumber for firewood. It was when they were thus employed that they had come upon the hatch for the companionway of a vessel apparently newly built. They had called out to him across the sands, "companion."

Since the companion had not been from the *Lark*, but from a much newer vessel, everyone had concluded that it had belonged to the mysterious brig they had last seen over the northwest bar. "If so," Philip had written in his journal, "all hands have perished."

* * *

One of the peculiarities about Sable Island which had always puzzled him was the way in which some wrecks were so quickly swallowed by quicksands and currents, leaving only small signs of their demise (like the companion of the unknown brig), whereas others, grounded in the same vicinity, had not broken up for ten or fifteen years or more.

Two vessels wrecked in Darby's time on the north shore not far from the principal station — the *Eliza* in 1840 and the

Detroit in 1846 — had still been salvageable in his own time. On slack days in his early years on the island Philip recalled the many times he had taken crews to remove copper from both these derelicts.

Yet expeditions to old wrecks and new had on a good many occasions turned up unwelcome surprises. All too often the wrecker's axe, splitting the timbers, had uncovered a builder's deception — sham metal fastenings, the use of a two- or three-inch piece of metal where the design called for a long bolt. To save money, the builder had jeopardized the safety of the vessel, knowing that until the ship broke up no evidence of his dishonesty would come to light.

Such a man was surely, Philip thought, more despicable by far than the early wreckers. Safe in his workshop, a trusted member of the community, he took no risks in fitting out the vessels he sold with useless fastenings.

Yet what had increasingly, over the years, distressed Philip most about the risky and difficult occupation of wrecking had been the dangers and discomforts to which the wreckers themselves had been subjected. Philip had certainly felt for those they had rescued and subsequently looked after; had been concerned too about salvaging the cargoes; but most of all he had been anxious about his men. He had been responsible for them. When to send them out through the surf? When to hold them back? Time after time the decision — a life and death decision — had been his.

For the passengers and crew taken off the doomed vessels the trauma was usually less drawn out than for their rescuers. Each survivor was got off in a single trip, whereas the lifeboatmen had to go back and forth to the wreck until the last person had been evacuated. Working under pressure day and night — sometimes for two or three days and nights, without rest or proper food, in punishing cold and wind and surf — had sometimes brought even the strongest and most balanced to the breaking point. Philip had worried that some day one or more of his men would be pushed beyond endurance. And just before Christmas 1864 this had happened. His worst fears had been realized.

The *William Bennett* had been caught in a gale in which she had lost her foretopmast and bowsprit. On December 19 she had anchored off the north side of the island and run up a distress signal. However, the surf had been too wild then for Philip and his men to venture out in. Helpless, they had watched from shore all day, waiting for a lull.

All the next day they had tried to get a line aboard, but the storm was still too violent. It had not been until evening — the evening of the 20th — that they had been able to get a line fast and start taking off crew and passengers. By this time Philip could see that his lifeboatmen were exhausted. He was himself.

However, they had all persevered. It had seemed as if there had been no alternative. And, one by one, everyone — even a baby — had been got off safely.

This had seemed a happy ending. At Main Station the women had bustled around serving up hot food and settling the survivors in warm beds.

During all this fuss over those who had been rescued, two of the lifeboatmen, Peter de Young and Henry Osborne, had slipped away. Philip, himself exhausted and feeling that everything that could be done had been, had fallen asleep.

The next day both Peter and Henry had been found — halfway home — dead. Their wet clothes were frozen like a shell around them.

Peter had expired halfway to his mother's house. He appeared to have lain down on the sand to rest.

Henry would not have perished if he had not first gone to check on his sister on the South Side. He had worried about her safety in the storm — needlessly, as it turned out — since, when he had reached her house, he had found everything safe. He had then set off at once for home. Next day his lifeless body had been found on the shore — halfway home.

They had buried the lifeboatmen on the island. The rest of the world had not even heard of their deaths for over three months — and then only glancingly at the end of a short newspaper account of the rescue of those aboard the *William Bennett* in the middle pages of the *Acadian Recorder*.

During this time the captain, crew and passengers of the *William Bennett* had had to stay put. The weather had continued too inclement for the *Daring* to get out to Sable. Until spring the lifeboats had operated with two men short . . . .

And despite all the burials he had presided over during his years on the island, Philip had never really gotten over the deaths of Peter de Young and Henry Osborne. If only he had insisted on their staying at Main Station that fatal night! He should have seen that they were not up to the trek home . . . .

* * *

Peter de Young — an able man, yet so unfortunate! Philip supposed that de Young had never really recovered from his wife's death on the *Daring*'s return trip to Halifax that mid-September day near the beginning of Philip's second year on the island. After that blow and the death of his child a few months later — Peter had appeared too careless of his own safety and well being, too ready to take risks.

Daly had told Philip about the sad business . . . about putting into Ship's Harbor for a coffin the day after Mrs. de Young's death . . . about how — although Walker and another willing and able carpenter had been on board — no suitable material for building such a box had been at hand . . . .

* * *

Daly and the *Daring*! Without him, wrecking on the island — the way it was done in the late fifties and early sixties anyway — would have been out of the question. It was not only that Daly and he had been the two constants year after year while the other men aboard the schooner and on the island had come and gone — and even the island itself had shifted position — but that Daly had again and again demonstrated such extraordinary stamina, courage and audacity. So many of Philip's memories of wrecking were tied up with this intrepid and sometimes ruthless man and the schooner whose name so aptly described a dominant facet of her master's character.

Daly had invariably seemed to sense when a storm was about to strike the island and throw up wreckage on its shores. Then, without hesitation, he would weigh anchor in Halifax Harbor and sail into the storm, ride it out in the vicinity of Sable Island, and appear — miraculously, it often seemed to Philip and his men — to anchor just off Main Station once the worst was over. Time after time, Philip remembered, Daly's crew had been in time to help his own island wreckers.

The wrecking of the *Eliza Ross* at the end of the first week of December 1856 had been such an instance. Philip and his men had just gotten Captain Muggah and his crew off the vessel when the *Daring* hove in sight.

What had made this occasion particularly memorable was partly that the *Daring* herself had only barely escaped foundering along with the *Eliza Ross*, and partly that Philip had learned how unbending — to the point of ruthlessness — Daly could sometimes be.

Daly's account of this near disaster aboard the *Daring* had jibed almost exactly with Captain Muggah's relation of **his** ship's demise. The dual accounts, together with his own observations of the salvaging of the *Eliza Ross* and Daly's treatment of his men during this and subsequent undertakings, had all contributed to the lasting impression. The strong emotions awakened in him at the time had been reactivated by a recent opportunity to reread Daly's log, written as events had unfolded.

* * *

Daly had not been far off Sable Island on December third when he had noted: "I have not seen the Barometer fall so fast for several years."

By the next day, he had reported: "A most furious Gale, almost a hurricane with one of the highest Seas I have seen for many years."

Daly had gone on to remark that "the Sea was most fearful," and then, subsequently, to report how the *Daring* had been struck on the port quarter by a sea which hove the vessel to wind . . . following which another sea struck her on the starboard bow, a blow which hove her completely round.

"I thought," Daly had noted in the log, "for the moment that the Vessel would go down stern foremost. Indeed, it was only the Almighty that saved us from such a fate." To the amazement of all, the vessel recovered herself and came to the wind on the starboard tack without receiving any injury.

Nevertheless, the reprieve had been temporary. "It was

92

blowing a Hurricane with a dreadful Sea," Daly had noted on the fifth. He had gone on to describe how the violence of the wind had been so intense that it had cut the tops off the waves, spewing water and foam into the air in a steady downpour. Daly, though the last men in the world one could imagine giving up, had observed at this juncture that he did not think the vessel could live through such a pummelling.

Convinced now that some — or all — of his men would be swept into the sea by the force of wind and water, Daly had ordered all hands below to the cabin, leaving only one man, strongly lashed, on deck at the wheel. Each time the *Daring* descended into a trough and rose again, Daly and his men had marvelled. "It is the admiration of all on board how the vessel lives," Daly had written.

By December 6 conditions were no better. If anything, they had worsened. Snow squalls had begun. "I hardly know what to do," Daly had admitted.

If Philip had not seen the words himself, he would never have believed that any power on earth could have drawn such an admission from Daly.

By suppertime of the same day, the men reported that the *Daring*'s stock of fuel was low. At 6 p.m. the fire in the galley had been extinguished, and by 8 p.m. the cabin fire was out. At midnight, with the temperature in the cabin near freezing, Daly reported that the weather outside was still stormy with snow squalls and a heavy sea.

During the next two days the *Daring* managed to ride out the remainder of the storm. By late on December 8 she was anchored off the island, and by the ninth had taken Captain Muggah and his crew on board for the return trip to Halifax.

Daly had now behaved as if the nightmare of the six preceding days had never been — as if the trip out had been like a routine summer crossing with calm seas and steady breezes . . . with his men warm, well fed and rested. Consequently, he had spared neither himself nor his men. None of them had had a chance to rest or have a proper meal. Instead, he had pushed forward with the procedures he ordinarily followed when a vessel had been wrecked on the island. He had ordered his men to participate in the salvaging of the *Eliza Ross*. And since they were more afraid of Daly's anger and recriminations if they refused than of the still wild sea and their precarious balance on the icy deck of the wrecked vessel, they had labored throughout the tenth day of December alongside the men of the Establishment.

The following day, Daly had summoned all his men on deck. On canvassing the provisions aboard the wrecked vessel, he announced, he had found that a barrel of bread had been opened, and that about two-thirds of the contents had been taken. Who, he inquired, had broken open the barrel and made off with the bread?

Each man denied any knowledge of the theft.

Daly had stormed and threatened to punish everyone on board unless the culprit confessed.

All hands remained silent.

Daly was quick to make good his promise. The verdict: every man was guilty . . . everyone would be punished.

Daly had at once meted out the punishment and recorded his actions in the *Daring*'s log: "Each person on board the vessel is to receive an allowance of three quarts of water per day until we reach the land . . . and also in consequence of daring to open any stores without my knowledge . . . an allowance of a pound of bread a day . . . ."

Depriving his men of food was, Philip knew, Daly's time-tried way of disciplining them. That Daly was inflexible in administering justice had been on numerous occasions the talk of the men of the Establishment. They swapped stories regularly with the crew of the *Daring* while loading and unloading supplies and salvaged goods.

So it was that everyone on the island heard about Daly's next disciplinary action . . . less than three months later.

During the first part of March, Daly, after being ashore on the mainland, had boarded the *Daring*, which was tied up at the wharf, and, not having seen a man on deck keeping the anchor watch, had asked the mate why. The mate had told Daly that everyone had refused to keep the watch.

True to form, Daly had at once called all hands, asking them their objections to keeping the usual anchor watch and the cause of their refusal to do so . . . .

Their answer: that after so long a time being tossed about at sea, they thought they would have a good night's rest

— and that, besides, they had only shipped to go to Sable Island and back.

Daly's breathless reply, delivered promptly as usual and recorded soon afterwards in his log: "I told them that they were as much bound to me as if they had shipped for seven years, and that I insisted on the watch being kept, and that unless it was kept . . . the vessel should remain in the harbor until I sent express to Halifax for another crew, and that I would not allow any provisions to be cooked on board for their use . . . ."

The men had subsequently "consented" to keep the watch, as Daly had noted. No emperor, Philip had thought, was ever more determined and surer of getting his own way than Daly. For although he had continued to lose crew and chronicle mutinous behavior aboard his vessel, he had always had the last word, as far as Philip knew.

However, the disciplinary action aboard the government schooner which had most closely touched Philip and the rest of the men at the Establishment had been Peter de Young's dismissal from the *Daring*.

After the death of his wife and child, Peter had wanted to get away from the island where everything reminded him of his losses. Such a reaction was understandable, Philip had felt. It was just that shipping on the *Daring* had not provided a satisfactory alternative.

For several years everything had gone smoothly enough. Peter had, indeed, once been laid off with a bad ankle, but Daly had taken him back after it had healed. The real difficulty had occurred one early August day when Peter had inadvertently displeased the *Daring's* master by washing a pair of canvas trousers on the quarter deck. When Daly had espied de Young, he had expressed his annoyance. Peter had, according to Daly, responded in a "rather impertinent" way, resenting the reprimand . . . or so Daly had thought.

Just over a fornight later, when the *Daring* docked in Halifax, Daly had discharged Peter . . . and, as a result of this dismissal, Peter had decided to return to Sable Island. Philip had been happy enough to have him back.

On the island, although everyone knew that the routines were harsh and often dangerous, no one was under full time surveillance as on the *Daring*. On Sable Island no commanding officer could keep tabs on everyone all the time — and in any case no one was likely to complain about where or when one washed one's trousers.

the fishery

". . . it becomes my duty to invite your Excellency's attention to the value of the Fishery upon its coast.

The countless schools of Mackarel [sic], which in spring pass our shores on their way to the eastward, and which annually resort to the gulf, pass between Sable Island and the main-land. In going, as in returning, they often trim its shores in vast quantities. The fall fish are very fine. During the three days I remained on the Island, except when they were driven off by the storm, there were seldom less than five or six schooners in sight, catching these fish with the hook and line. All the vessels similarly engaged made, I believe, full fares. The Superintendant (McKenna) informed me that a few days before the *Daring* arrived, the Mackarel [sic] crowded the coast in such numbers that they almost pressed each other upon the sands, and I saw an unbroken school, extending, near the landing place, for a mile in length, within good seining distance, besides others at various points, indicating the presence, in the surrounding seas, of incalculable wealth.

With a good seine, or two, I have no doubt that the Island crew could, on the day I landed, or on the day I left, have stopped one thousand barrels, and, if so, it is clear that no salvage obtained from wrecks, and no profits from pasturage, or the cultivation of the soil, would yield to the government so rich a return for a little judicious outlay, as this valuable fishery . . . ."

— Joseph Howe, "Report on Sable Island," October 21, 1850.

Howe's proposal for developing Sable Island into a large and thriving fishing station was, Philip had realized soon after his arrival, even more impractical than Judge Haliburton's earlier scheme for placing a thousand families on Scatarie to fish. It was not that fish were not present in immense numbers in both locations. The problem was pulling them in safely from shore bases. On Sable Island only the seals had figured out how to do this.

Here, getting out through the surf was a problem nearly every day of the year. Howe had indeed mentioned, glancingly, the difficulties fishermen might experience at times due to the height and force of the breakers, but, as these had not been a serious deterrent to his getting to and from the *Daring* during his three-day sojourn on the island, he had not considered them to be insuperable obstacles the other three hundred and sixty-two.

Moreover, since he had seen American fishing schooners hauling in full fares off Sable Island, Howe had not understood why Nova Scotian vessels should not do as well. Indeed, with a base on the island, they should do better.

But Howe had not had Philip's first-hand and long-term experience with the fisheries of Nova Scotia. He had not had the disparities between the American and Nova Scotian fishing fleets brought home to him time out of mind as Philip had. If Nova Scotian fishing captains could not compete with their American counterparts in the relatively tranquil and close-to-home waters off Port Hood, how, Philip had wanted to ask, could they hope to cope at all in the turbulent North Atlantic off Sable Island? There, they would be out of sight of hospitable land — indeed, the better part of a hundred miles off Cape Canso, the nearest mainland outcropping.

Moreover, Philip had wanted to point out — as he and other fisheries' officers had already done on many occasions several years earlier — that neither the inferior construction of most of the native fishing vessels nor their awkward and antiquated equipment made them suitable for ventures which would take them well out from their home ports. Encouraging such voyages without improving the caliber of the fishing boats would, Philip had reckoned, only add to the numbers of vessels foundering off Sable Island.

Here then was another instance of foolish government suggestions being made about the running of an island outpost whose workings no politician or bureaucrat — even a perspicacious and imaginative one like Joe Howe — could understand in the course of a three-day visit.

Howe, for instance, clearly had had no idea how much

time the farming, building and salvaging took; and consequently, how very little time, even if conditions had been ideal, could ever be allotted to fishing. As it was, there were too few men to make the rounds and do the work. Why Howe had not even mentioned recruiting and sending out the contingent of fishermen which would be necessary for the carrying out of such an enterprise. As things had stood during his superintendency, Philip had thought himself lucky to get out fishing two or three times a year — and then the Establishment could only spare one, or occasionally two men to accompany him.

Howe had arrived at a slack time. The planting and harvesting were over, and no new wrecks had been thrown up upon the sands. Without actually participating in the island's routines day after day, year round, it was impossible for a visitor to imagine how much time the ordinary work took.

He himself had, he realized now, been slow to understand the endless labor and frustrations of a Humane Establishment. Long before he had come to Sable Island, when he had anchored the *Sylph* or the *Responsible* off the little harbor at Scatarie and gone ashore to visit James, he had never seriously considered the workings of that Establishment. He had taken some notice of the tasks in hand, but only, he had realized later, in a superficial way. One had to live the life to understand it properly. Only since his own years on Sable had he realized what sort of life James had lived on Scatarie.

* * *

Despite the commercial advantages Howe and others had foreseen from a fishery operating from Sable Island, Philip was not for it. Such an enterprise would, he was convinced, be counterproductive to the work of the Establishment.

Fishermen would never, he felt sure, be governed by the rules. Each fishing captain would do exactly as he pleased. All his years as fisheries and revenue officer had provided the basis for such a judgement, and his subsequent years on Sable Island had substantiated it. Fishermen generally, and American fishermen in particular, were a law onto themselves.

Of all the visitors to the island during his superintendency, Philip had found that by far the most consistently troublesome had been the fishermen — the majority of them New Englanders. Unlike most others who had turned up on Sable Island, the fishermen were generally in control of their landings. Anchored within sight of land and surreptitious in their movements, they could bide their times and choose their locations to come ashore.

They rarely appeared near the principal station, or indeed near any of the inhabited houses. Instead, they made for the house of refuge, where, time out of mind, they had plundered the stores left there for shipwrecked survivors.

Usually the fishermen had put to sea before there could be a confrontation. But if one of the patrol happened upon them in the midst of such a theft, well, he was only one man against two or three or more. And by the time the Establishment employee could return to Main Station to report the incident, the intruders had gone.

It was, Philip was sure, no accident that the first wreckers were said to be fishermen, and that their dreadful reputations for lawlessness and destructiveness had led to the founding of the Establishment. Such men would, Philip surmised, never dream of risking their lives in such a dangerous environment for humanitarian reasons or for the marginal returns he and his men received. The fishermen would always, he was sure, be more interested in quick returns and in what they could get for themselves than in helping others. They did not, moreover, seem to care about leaving anything for the next comer — neither supplies in the house of refuge nor creatures in the ocean.

History, Philip felt, had shown the result of the fishermen's greed. By the turn of the century they had killed off all the sea cows or walruses, hundreds of which had frequented the island from time immemorial. At one point they had almost finished off the wild horses too, killing more than they needed for meat.

But it was on the banks off Sable Island that Philip had himself observed the fishermen's single-minded destructiveness. They had systematically fished out the best grounds.

House of refuge on the lake.
Dr. Gilpin, 1854. Admiral Digby Library and Historical Society

James Farquhar on patrol
Dr. Gilpin, 1854

The depletion of one of these, Bank Quereau,* just northeast of Sable, had in fact occurred since his arrival on the island. French and American fishermen had vied with one another on this bank, spoiling it altogether by set line fishing. There were, as one observer noted, "hundreds of vessels, thousands of men and millions of hooks employed in taking codfish with set lines." By 1860, five years after his arrival, Bank Quereau had been ruined — or so the government records showed .... And yet, in 1873 when he was preparing to leave Sable Island, Philip had observed that the Americans were still visible offshore in large numbers — fishing.

---

* Now written Banquereau.

visitors

"Toiling through the deep and yielding sand they (visitors) plod slowly through the ravine, and presently turn into a broad, grassy valley, sheltered by lofty hills which completely shut them in from the ocean. Here, ranged around an irregular square, are the several buildings of the principal station — the comfortable house of the Superintendent, where a hospitable welcome always awaits the stranger, be he casual visitor or castaway; the Sailors' Home for shipwrecked crews; substantial quarters for the men; two or three large stores and boat-houses; the blacksmith's shop, oil-house, and outbuildings. There is also a well-stocked barn and barnyard, where one may hear the low of kine and the cackle of domestic fowls. There are pigs and horses, and a garden neatly inclosed. And conspicuous over all, on a neighboring hill, towers the flag-staff and crow's-nest, from which the entire Island can be scanned at a glance in clear weather. Just in front of the little hamlet, and down a sloping beach, a boat lies tranquilly at anchor on the bosom of a lake which stretches away to the right and left for fifteen miles, in varying outline of shore. So sudden and complete is the transition from the former scene that one might fancy himself in some sequestered inland vale but for the eternal roar of the surf dinning in his ears."

— C. Halleck, "The Secrets of Sable Island," in *Harper's New Monthly Magazine* (December, 1866).

Halleck had been only one of the hundreds of visitors who had, willingly or unwillingly, come to Sable during Philip's superintendency and accepted the hospitality of the Establishment. Like several earlier callers who had chosen to pay a visit to the island, had stayed there briefly and been at once captivated by its wild beauty and appalled by its grisly reputation, Halleck had felt compelled on his return home to jot down his impressions. In doing so he had, Philip reflected,

The Principal Station
Dr. Gilpin, 1854.

accurately depicted the natural environment, while making several mistakes about the island's history and its contemporary residents. Chief among these, Philip had thought, had been the report of his own death!

However, in the end, the words in Halleck's article which had continued to bother him had been the journalist's depiction of him as superintendent — as an out-of-shape, rather grim and vain old man. The words had stayed with him for years — were still with him, in fact: a "portly old sea dog" with "grim and rugged features and iron-grey locks" who "with pardonable vanity was wont to decorate himself with the medals and rewards of worthy service which he had so justly won . . . ."

The description seemed unfair. Could this pompous and grim old sea dog, bedecked with medals, be himself, Philip? True, Halleck had seen him chiefly on formal occasions when he had presided over dinner and prayers — not when he had been engaged in the physically or emotionally demanding routines of the Establishment. Yet, Philip had been left with the uncomfortable feeling that, if any impressions of himself survived for posterity, Halleck's would likely be all there were. The people who had known and understood him best would not write about him. Or was he vain even to think about posterity?

Halleck had been lodged in Philip' house at Main Station. Generally, in keeping with a long-established island tradition, such educated and upper class visitors stayed at Headquarters, in the superintendent's house, providing, of course, that there was room.

Ordinary seamen and less distinguished visitors were billeted in the houses (and sometimes even the barns) closest to the spot they had come ashore. Sometimes the Farquhars at the East End House or the Knocks at the South Side Station had put up entire crews of wrecked vessels for months. Amazingly, they had coped, despite the demands of their own large families. They had not even appeared to mind: open-handed hospitality to unexpected guests had seemed an understood prerequisite for staff of any of the stations of the Sable Island Establishment.

Philip had found that most of the visitors under his roof had worried a good deal about getting off the island. Those who arrived in the autumn were the touchiest. They had, it seemed, no sooner landed than they began to fret about being stranded on Sable for the winter. This was particularly true of those who had been brought to the island to do a specific job. These men tended, Philip had observed, to work somewhat frantically, with one eye on their timepieces and the other on the weather. Most memorable for him amongst these working visitors had been John Campbell and his crew who had been sent out to prospect for gold, and James Kerr who had supervised the building of the lighthouses.

In 1857 Philip had written to Hugh Bell suggesting that experts be sent to Sable to determine whether there was enough gold in the island's sands to make recovering these precious grains worthwhile. Since gold was a magic word, his request for knowledgeable prospectors had produced a quicker and more positive response than many of the more mundane demands he had presented to the Board of Works.

By early October the following year Campbell and two

helpers had been dispatched to Sable Island. They had stayed ten days and clearly been pleased to leave at the end of that time.

Nevertheless, they had returned in 1859, even later in the season — at the end of December, in fact — apparently eager to continue their work. The lure of gold had seemed as certain to hold fear at bay on the sands of Nova Scotia's remotest outpost as in the wilderness of British Columbia's interior.

By the early sixties another team had been given permission to prospect on the island. Its members too seemed hopeful that the shore washings would yield grains of gold comparable in value to those found in the beach sands at The Ovens.

William Cunard had become wealthy from this venture alone. A Cunard vessel had been kept busy for months transporting men and supplies and carrying the precious metal back to Halifax.

For the Cunards, and for Philip too, the prospect of sifting gold from beach sand had been a far cry from the mining ventures they had all been involved in previously. Supervising the hacking of coal from Cape Breton's rocky headlands had been quite another business. However, whether coal or gold, Philip had remained a manager. It was men like the Cunards who had made the fortunes from both.

* * *

But to get back to the reluctant visitors. . . .

James Kerr's eagerness to leave Sable Island had been more pronounced than the prospectors' — but then, of course, he had been detained there longer and things had not gone so smoothly.

For his final visit Kerr had landed the last day of April 1873. (Philip remembered the particulars of this visit well because it had taken place so recently and because he had found Kerr compatible.)

During most of May, Kerr had seemed content enough. Work on the west end lighthouse had proceeded well. Indeed Kerr had predicted cheerfully that by midsummer this second lighthouse would be much further advanced than its counterpart on the east end had been at the same time the preceding year.

Then several hitches had occurred. The first, minor and scarcely out of the ordinary, had only dampened his enthusiasm; the second, major and unexpected, had completely extinguished it.

Kerr's early frustration on the island had had to do with being unable to get letters to and from the mainland. Like Philip himself, Kerr had a daughter to whom he was particularly devoted and to whom he wrote regularly. In late May the government steamer had been spotted off the island, but then had not arrived at Main Station. Instead, the vessel had anchored some fifteen miles away and remained there very briefly. Being short of coal, as they had learned later, she had been obliged to return at once to Halifax. Kerr had, consequently had to wait to send his letters on the *Lady Head*'s next trip.

Although Philip himself was enured to such happenings, he and Susannah had remarked that their guest's disappointment had been strong and prolonged. They had thought this somewhat surprising. A former seafaring man, indeed a seizing officer like Philip himself, might, they thought, have been expected to take such occurrences in his stride.

They had been more understanding of Kerr's reaction to what had happened some ten days later: namely, the toppling of a portion of the new lighthouse. It had fallen during the night, and, as Kerr had observed tersely, would require some time to replace . . . .By early July Kerr had been heard to remark that he intended leaving Sable Island before winter whether the lighthouse was finished or not.

Philip could accept this point of view. He had made the same decision himself.

* * *

Not all the reluctant visitors to Sable Island during Philip's tenure there had been human. For him the most memorable and sympathetic of the animal transients had been the horse Napoleon.

107

Imported into Nova Scotia in 1854, Napoleon had been one of nine stud stallions purchased in Canada and the United States for the purpose of upgrading the horse population throughout the province. A committee of the House had assigned Napoleon to Cape Breton and Victoria counties, and it was from there that he had been sent to Sable Island.

Philip had felt more for this imported horse than for any of the native island breed, perhaps because, like himself, Napoleon had been a stranger on the island during his own first winter there. For both of them the winter of 1855-'56 had been trying. The harsh new environment, together with the traumatic landing in a lifeboat, had taken some getting used to for strangers from "away," and the government had not been very understanding of the hardships either horse or man had had to put up with. Its members had not given either one time to acclimatize himself before making unreasonable demands.

The stud horse had, like other expected visitors, arrived and departed on the *Daring*, although with more commotion. At the time Philip had not been used to the brutality of shipping horses from Sable Island.

In fact, he never quite accustomed himself to the procedure. Getting the poor brutes onto the *Daring* or other vessels for the one-way crossing to the mainland had, throughout his tenure, seemed a cruel and punishing business. But whereas the native ponies had had to put up with a single crossing to the mainland, poor Napoleon had endured two trips on the *Daring* in less than a year. And on his return trip he was, after a winter in the open, in poor condition. He was not fit to travel.

Philip had wanted to hold off until late summer when the horse would have been in peak form. If Napoleon had been his, the noble and spirited creature would have stayed put till then. But the members of the House committee had been impatient about getting their property off the island in early spring. Napoleon, they seemed to think, could be trussed up and got off as readily as any other item stored on the island over the winter.

No one in Halifax, Philip had often thought, had ever seemed much concerned about the conditions under which the Sable Island horses were shipped. Even in 1852 when some sixteen out of forty horses had died on the journey to Newfoundland not much had been said.

A number of times during that first winter Philip had tried to catch Napoleon or at least lure him into one of the barns for a good feed and a rest. But the stud horse had withstood his advances. He had quickly become as reluctant as the native island ponies he ran with to relinquish his freedom. Like the other stallions, Napoleon had simply snorted and turned tail at the close approach of any human being.

Even by mid-May Philip had not succeeded in rounding up the now wild horse, and he had had to send a letter of apology to Halifax in place of the stallion, together with firm promises that Napoleon would be caught, bound and delivered on the *Daring*'s next crossing. He had kept his word reluctantly.

By June of 1857, the year following Napoleon's return to civilization, Philip had been able to report to Hugh Bell that there were some very promising foals on the island. Yet by the fall of that same year, Philip had expressed a reluctance to ship any of the island horses. He could not have mustered a reasonable cargo. McKenna, Philip felt, had been too enthusiastic about sending off large numbers of the best horses in his final year as superintendent.

And so, by the autumn of 1857, Philip had noted that the old mares were failing. No one, he had pointed out to his superiors, would be interested in buying them; nor were they suitable for producing an outstanding crop of new foals on the island. As for the young mares, shipping them would have been disastrous as far as improvement of the island breed was concerned. Napoleon's visit would have been for naught. Philip's argument had, on this occasion, carried the day.

* * *

Elley had liked Napoleon's offspring. She had liked the native horses and the seals too, responding perhaps to the free and exuberant life which was so apparent in these wild creatures. But then, responding positively had always been typical of Elley; and, Philip had thought since, it had perhaps been partly because of his daughter's spontaneous and

Transporting the small lake boat
Dr. Gilpin, 1854. Admiral Digby Library and Historical Society.

enthusiastic reaction to life on Sable Island that he had himself been able to come to terms with it. She had certainly been his favorite visitor.

Elley had arrived for her first visit in mid-November near the beginning of his second year as superintendent. She had been one of the few rays of sunshine in the otherwise dark months following McIsaac's insubordination.

It was on a Saturday, just past noon and exceedingly calm, when he had spotted the *Daring* and sent the lifeboat out. The almost total absence of surf was always a surprise in midsummer, but in November it had seemed a miracle. Yet no sooner had Elley got up to Main Station and exclaimed over its cosy situation behind the dunes, than the snow had begun to fall. By late afternoon the wind had risen and a gale raged. The surf had pounded with renewed fury, as if the lull of the early afternoon had given it increased energy.

Small boat on Sable Island's lake
Dr. Gilpin, 1854. Admiral Digby Library and Historical Society

Although Philip remembered this visit most clearly, there had been many others. Elley had come in fine weather too — had gone boating down the lake looking for gulls' eggs, had gone clamming and lobstering, had sketched and painted . . . .

He and Susannah had counted on these regular visits. They had not realized how much until they had stopped. Elley had surprised them both, announcing that she would marry Cotton Mather Almon and move West with him. Philip and Susannah had in some ways been pleased with this news, but, at the same time, their lives had seemed, all at once, narrower. The life which had connected them most strongly to one another and to the mainland had moved out of their orbit. They had both felt cut off, stranded.

Sable Island scene
Elley Dodd, 1869. (PANS N-4641)

departure — December 1873

"I hope you are settled in your *Government* and that you may long enjoy your health to fill the office to which you are entitled and (to) which you are best adapted of all my friends."

— from a letter from J.B. Uniacke to Philip Dodd, written November 10, 1855

* * *

"It is very hard to have such a gang on Sable Island as are there now . . . ."

— James Daly, from the log of the *Daring,* December 13, 1855

* * *

"The condition of the Humane Establishments on our coasts I am sorry to say are not such as they should be and reflect but little credit on Nova Scotia that has the control of them."

— From M.D. McKenna's report, from the office of the Board of Works, on lighthouses and Humane Establishments, September 1863

* * *

"A new lighthouse and fog whistle for the east end of Sable Island is now in full operation. Another lighthouse which is being constructed at the west end will be completed next February. It will be 70 feet high and the most powerful light on the coast of America."

— from the Halifax *Reporter*, November 9, 1872

From first to last his time on Sable had been a series of ups and downs. Now it was time to leave.

Looking back over his eighteen years as Governor or the island, Philip thought that the achievements and the setbacks had pretty much balanced out. Despite the building of the much-talked-about lighthouses — the most powerful on the coasts of America, they said — he was no longer so convinced of their absolute and enduring worth, or of his own. If the shifting sands of this place had anything to teach, it was that nothing much about life was permanent, assured or settled.

Even a good many people he had thought he could depend on had not stood firmly behind him. Friends like Uniacke had indeed supported him unequivocally from the first, expressing total confidence in his ability to govern his island domain: yet others like Daly had from time to time criticized his rule, blaming him when they were themselves inconvenienced. It had been the censure, not the praise, which he had brooded over.

Philip still recalled how exasperated Daly had been that first December when he had wanted to land supplies, and the Establishment's boat had not come out promptly to get them. Daly, as Philip had been told later, had sat fuming as the anchored *Daring* had been buffeted by wind and waves. Daly, as he eventually told anyone who would listen, had signalled his readiness to land the provisions he had brought from Halifax, and then not been answered by the island's signal post. At length, as Daly told the story, he had observed through his glass the island's boat being made ready for launching — and then, unbelievably, pulled back from the surf at the last moment.

His own men, as Daly had at this point in his recital remarked eagerly, had then offered to go ashore in the *Daring's* boat. They had, he stressed, not been afraid. Why then, he asked, had Philip's men been so hesitant about setting out in the Establishment's lifeboat — a far superior craft, and one designed especially for Sable Island's surf?

For Philip this had seemed a slap in the face. Yet what had really rankled had been Daly's intimation that McKenna would have understood his signal and answered it — and that

114

McKenna would also not have hesitated to launch the lifeboat . . . . Worst of all, Philip had had to admit to himself that Daly had probably been right. McKenna had obviously known what he was doing, had apparently been able to gauge as exactly as was possible the right time to act . . . whereas he, Philip, during those first few months, had not yet learned to assess altogether accurately the idiosyncrasies of the island, the fluctuating conditions of the surf, or the abilities and dispositions of the men under him.

McKenna! Always McKenna! He had been constantly, from beginning to end, a shadowy, supervisory figure in the background — or so it had seemed. McKenna! Forever opinionated and judgemental!

There had, of course, been all that trouble with McIsaac at the beginning; but halfway through his term of office, just when Philip had been able to put the unpleasantness well behind him, McKenna had come up with new reproaches. What had he meant exactly about Nova Scotia's Humane Establishments doing the province little credit?

Perhaps McKenna's oblique remarks had merely been directed at the light stations of St. Paul's and Scatarie where he had been eager to have Gesner's new oil — albertine* (or kerosene) substituted for whale oil. Certainly that had been a real preoccupation of McKenna's about this time. He had, Philip knew, preached with evangelical fervor on this subject, and indeed converted John Kendrick and others at the Board of Works.

Or maybe McKenna had had the wretched lifeboats at St. Paul's and Scatarie uppermost in his mind. If he had, he would, Philip agreed, have been right. Daly, when he had taken Jacob Miller, McKenna's predecessor, to check on the light stations and Humane Establishments, had been appalled by the condition of the boats which had put out to the *Daring*. And Scatarie's lifeboat, Philip knew, was almost identical to St. Paul's. Scatarie and St. Paul's had from the beginning been provided with identical facilities. Edmund and Sam Cunard had made a point of this.

---

* Gesner gave it this name because he discovered it in Albert County, New Brunswick.

But Philip could not help wondering whether McKenna had really been making general criticisms of St. Paul's, Scatarie and the others — or had Sable been uppermost in his mind? Since the Board of Works in Halifax presided over such a handful of Humane Establishments, and since Sable Island's was the largest and most notable, it was difficult, Philip thought, for that island's governor not to take McKenna's condemnation personally.

This time, as before, McKenna had not come forward to explain. Consequently, the air had not been cleared. Philip had been left to ponder how he could better govern his island: He had not come up with any new or startling ideas. Just keeping things going had proved increasingly hard. He was, he supposed, tired. He felt as if he had had enough.

And this last year, 1873, had in every way been among the busiest and most frustrating of his governorship. Not only had work on the lighthouses complicated the routine activities, but on no other year since his arrival had more vessels gone aground on the island.

Increasingly, he had the nagging fear that McKenna had been right about *not* having lighthouses on Sable Island. And although McKenna no longer held sway in the Board of Works office — had indeed long since gone back to Shelburne County where he belonged — it had seemed to Philip (who counted himself as by no means a superstitious person) that McKenna's censorious presence had continued to hover over Sable Island until the instant Philip and Susannah had boarded the *Lady Head* for their return to Sydney.

VI

Epilogue

"Round the decay
Of that colossal wreck, boundless and bare
The lone and level sands stretch far away."

— Percy Bysshe Shelley (*Ozymandias*)

In 1882 the sands of time ran out for Philip Sherwood
Dodd. The same year, Sable Island's west end lighthouse
— hailed less than a decade before as the largest and finest on
the coasts of Nova Scotia — was inundated by the sea. By then
the surf and currents had torn away the shoals which had
formed off the west end about 1850. The gales of 1881 had
swept away the island's sands to within some fifteen feet of the
lighthouse; and the storms of 1882 had sucked the sand from
under the building, leaving it tilted and forlorn — a derelict.
The men of the establishment saved the mechanism, but
months went by before it could be installed in a new lighthouse.

During this time no light showed on Sable Island's west
end. And while the new lighthouse was abuilding, many of
those who had kept close tabs on the Sable Island
establishment over the years remarked that neither light on
Sable Island seemed to have made much difference to the
number of vessels foundering there. In the decade before the
building of the lighthouses and the decade afterwards, there
had been nearly the same number of wrecks. The lights, it

Sable Island sands
Dr. Gilpin, 1854. Admiral Digby Library and Historical Society

would seem, had neither lured unsuspecting mariners onto the island, as early detractors had feared; nor had they, apparently, been seen in time by captains disoriented in fog, or snow or driving rain.

* * *

Philip Dodd died at the age of 76 and was buried in St. George's churchyard, Sydney. His grave was just two removed from that of his son, also Philip Sherwood, the promising boy who had died so tragically in Bridgeport in December 1848 at

118

the age of 13 years, 8 months. Both graves bear identical crests and their inscriptions are among the clearest in the ancient churchyard. The grave of Philip Sherwood Dodd, Sr. is the first the modern visitor happens upon when he enters St. George's Church burial ground. Most of his companions here are the men and women and children he had known during his lifetime. The surviving markers, like his own, belong chiefly to Sydney's early elite. Only Edmund is commemorated inside the church, distinguished from his brothers and sisters in death as in life.

Yet some of the closest family members are missing — James, who wore himself out saving hapless mariners on Scatarie, and Philip's beloved daughter, Elley, who lived a long life and remained in death, as in life, with the family she had married into, the Almons.

In 1875 Elley, then 39, had surprised and delighted both the Dodds and the Almons by giving birth to a son, William Bruce, who was to become the fifth, and last, of the distinguished medical men of Halifax bearing the Almon name to dominate their profession in this city. William Bruce was born in Manitoba where Elley and her husband, Cotton Mather, then lived.

Philip's wife, the former Susannah Weston Haire, lived to hear of their grandson's birth. She died in April 1876, having been "poorly," the family agreed, since her return from Sable Island. Indeed, she had, everyone said, never recovered from the death of their son, nearly thirty years earlier.

In July 1876, several months after Susannah's death, Philip's brother Edmund had died at the age of 79, his death hastened by the tragic demise of his young son, Rupert Davenport, the previous October. The young man had been only 25 and this time Edmund had been inconsolable . . . Rupert was the fourth of his children to have died prematurely.

In 1882, the year of Philip's own death, Elley and her husband had returned to Halifax with the children. Cotton Mather was ill and they had all stayed at his father's home, *Rosebank*, hoping for a miraculous recovery. Cotton Mather, had, however, died a few months after her father (in March 1883) and Elley had been left to bring up their three children alone.

Philip in those last months had had the pleasure of seeing his grandchildren now and then, and of entertaining them, several of their visiting cousins, and anyone else who turned up, with a tune on his fiddle, that lifelong companion and consoler. And perhaps most of all because of these final tuneful interludes, Philip Sherwood Dodd was chiefly remembered by his surviving family as a "jolly old gentleman."

Yet there were others outside the family circle who retrospectively, registered their impressions of Philip Dodd. One of these was James Farquhar, a boy of thirteen whose father (named James Farquhar too) had presided over the east end station when Philip had arrived on Sable Island. He remembered the then newly-appointed superintendent as "a fine gentleman, an excellent shot and a good sportsman." Such a description might suggest that here indeed was a typical Victorian gentleman, a member of the squirearchy perhaps, brought up to do little except swank and hunt.

But although Philip Dodd could certainly hold his own in society, as well as with horse and gun, these were probably his most superficial accomplishments. He was, as the uncovered facts of his life show, just such a "Gentleman of Respectability and Character . . . also a man of Business" as Sir John Wentworth had originally intended placing in charge of his Humane Establishment. He was not an ordinary person tempted solely by "an offer of Pay and Provisions," but an exceptional individual with a strong sense of commitment. Not only did he carry out his duties on Sable Island with the same courage and integrity he had displayed earlier on the fisheries and revenue cutters, but in one year at least (1864) he even managed to turn a profit for the Establishment.

Despite such dedication and selflessness, with Philip Dodd's death, the struggles and voyages, the conflicts and accomplishments of his life were all but forgotten for more than a century. The memories of his life, like vessels which came to rest on Sable Island, were drifted over by the sands of time. Recently uncovered, they give the contemporary viewer both strangely dated and oddly fascinating insights.

For Philip Dodd belonged to a breed of principled brave and often lonely people who presided over Nova Scotia's offshore islands for 200 years. These men and women, these island keepers, dedicated many of the best years of their lives to rescuing other human beings they did not even know. Today their places are mostly filled by mechanical devices which, although they warn seafarers of shoals and other obstacles, cannot provide the comfort or the helping hand given so often by the former guardians of these out-of-the-way places.

On Scatarie Island the lighthouses are now automated. Robert Spears, the last keeper of the light which James Dodd first presided over, was pensioned off in 1987. No evidence of the Humane Establishment remains.

On Sable Island, although the lights there too are automated and the Humane Establishment closed down, human residents are still present. A handful of government supervisors, visiting scientists and artists continue to observe and record this island's changing patterns with the same sort of attentiveness that Dr. Gilpin and others brought to bear on this remote spot more than a century ago. So far they have been no more successful than their predecessors in preventing the waning of this intriguing sand crescent.

Appendix A

Dates and Facts Pertaining to this Account

1784   Cape Breton declared a province, separate from the rest of Nova Scotia, with its own capital, governor, and governing council.

1785   Governor DesBarres' founding of Sydney, the capital of the new province of Cape Breton. Richard Gibbons' appointment as chief justice of this new province.

1787   Governor DesBarres recalled to England for financial mismanagement. Landed on the Island of Jersey. Lieutenant Colonel William Macarmick installed in his stead.

1788   Marriage of Archibald Charles Dodd and Susannah Gibbons, daughter of Chief Justice Richard Gibbons.

1789   Start of the French Revolution.

1790   Birth of Archibald Charles and Susannah Gibbons Dodd's first child, William Charles Macarmick Dodd.

1791   Completion of St. George's Chapel, Sydney, by the military garrison.

1794   Capture of Chief Justice Richard Gibbons, his wife and son, Richard, by the French frigate *Tribune* in

the English Channel; and Chief Justice Gibbons'
subsequent death in a French prison.

1795   Birth of James Richard Dodd.

1796   Return to Sydney of Richard Gibbons Jr. (son of
Chief Justice Gibbons and brother of Susannah
Dodd).

1797   Birth of Edmund Murray Dodd.

"The total number of inhabitants (in Sydney) was
121, of whom about 26 were preparing to emigrate,
and when these should have left there would not be a
single person in the town except those who had
salaries to subsist upon — not a tailor, shoemaker,
smith, butcher — not even a washerwoman." (from
a report by a member of the governing council.)

1801   Inauguration of the world's first "Humane Estab-
lishment" (a life saving station) on Sable Island by
Governor Wentworth, on the recommendation of
John Howe.

1804   Napoleon made Emperor of the French.

1806   Birth of Philip Sherwood Dodd.

1810   James and Edmund Dodd joined the Royal Navy as
midshipmen.

1812   Beginning of war with the United States. Capture of
Edmund and James Dodd by the Americans.

1818   "By the terms of the convention of 1818, the United
States expressly renounced any right of fishing
within three marine miles from the coasts of these
colonies [on the Atlantic coast of British North
America], or of entering their bays, creeks and
harbors, except for shelter, or for wood and water."

1819   "The ship *Asia,* from the isle of Wight, with
detachments of artillery, and of the 15, 60, 62 and
74th regiments, struck on the N.W. reef of Sable
Island, in hazy weather, at 5 a.m., on the 2nd of
June. At noon she was apparently about 4 miles

from the island. By great exertions all on board were saved. Mrs. Mosse and child, Mrs. Almon, Miss Almon (belonging to Halifax), and the wives and children of officers and men were among the passengers. Some officers, who left the ship in her pinnace, with women and children, could not gain the island, but were rescued at sea by the American schooner *Phoebe and Sally*, Stephen Howes, master, from Boston. On this occasion the utility of the establishment was obvious, as without it a lingering death by hunger would probably have awaited the crew and passengers." (Murdoch)

1820   Cape Breton reannexed to Nova Scotia, largely due to the stormy and disastrous misrule by successive military governors. Charles Archibald Dodd and Edmund Murray Dodd struggled against reannexation.

End of reign of George III.

1824   Publication of Captain Joseph Darby's map of Sable Island.

1826   Edmund Murray Dodd married Mary Ann Sarah Weeks (on August 10).

Their son Archibald Otto born in October.

1827   Mining recommenced at Bridgeport.

1828   Death of Mary Ann Sarah Dodd (aged 24), wife of Edmund Murray Dodd.

1829   Revised version of Darby's Map of Sable Island.
1830   The General Mining Association (G.M.A.) began operating the Bridgeport colliery on Indian Bay 12 miles from Sydney, near the site where the French had dug coal for Louisbourg a century earlier.

1831   Edmund Murray Dodd married Caroline Maria Ritchie (on February 11).

Death of A.C. Dodd.

Samuel Cunard's visit to Seal Island in his capacity of lighthouse commissioner to see about setting up a Humane Establishment there.

1832   Election of Edmund Murray Dodd as member for Sydney in the Nova Scotia House of Assembly.

Increased immigration to Upper and Lower Canada as well as Nova Scotia. Most vessels set their course for Scatarie Island, the first landfall.

1833   Edmund Dodd (on March 19) petitioned the House on behalf of Daniel Shea of Sydney for money the latter had spent providing for castaways; as well as for the Sydney surgeons, Drs. Haire and Grey for treatments — particularly amputations of frost-bitten limbs — of mariners and passengers wrecked off Cape Breton.

During 1833 and 1834 ten vessels were lost on or near Scatarie Island. The total tonnage was 2766 and the number of people lost or rescued was 603. Eight of the rescuers subsequently filed claims at Sydney through Edmund Dodd for a total of £263 0 6, payable from the provincial treasury.

A 'House' committee (Edmund Dodd and James Uniake being among the 7 members) recommend "the necessity of a Light House on the Island of Scatarie, near the island of Cape Breton."

1834   From a report on lighthouses presented to the House: "The lighthouses in the United States are all lit with Sperm Oil, and in England, where Gas is not used, Sperm Oil is invariably substituted. It is said our lights are inferior to those of England, and in the United States; this is easily accounted for in both countries, as before mentioned, they burn the best of Spermaceti Oil at the cost in England of Six Shillings Sterling per Gallon and Five Shillings currency in the United States, whereas we have in use, Pale Seal Oil, at Two Shillings and Four pence half-penny per Gallon, not half the cost in either case, and surely it would be unreasonable to expect the same brilliant Light from an article so much inferior in quality and less in price . . ."

"Emigration of Colliers from the Mother Country to these Mines [at Bridgeport, Cape Breton] within the last four or five years has been extensive."

(June 12) Edward C. Bown of Sydney filed a petition — supported by 20 prominent citizens of Sydney, including Richard Gibbons — asking to be appointed keeper of the new lighthouse to be built on Scatarie Island.

Edmund Dodd presented the House with a claim of £263 0 6 (a sum considered exorbitant at the time), filed by 8 ships' captains for rescuing stranded mariners near Scatarie.

(December 23 and 24) "Ordered, that Mr. Dodd [Edmund] have leave of absence from the house to return home on urgent business."

(Monday, December 29) "At St. John's, Nfld. by Rev. F.G. Carrington Mr. Philip Dodd, Sydney, Cape Breton, married Susannah, second daughter of the late Mr. Alexander Haire." (*Halifax Journal*)

1835 (January 19) £500 set aside for Scatarie lighthouse.

(February 18 & 19) "On a motion of Mr. Uniacke, resolved that the same committee wait upon his Excellency the Lieutenant Governor, during the recess, and respectfully request his Excellency to call the attention of His Majesty's Government to the necessity of erecting a Light House on the Island of Scattarie [sic] near the County of Cape Breton."

James R. Dodd and his boat crew stationed on Scatarie during the shipping season to rescue human beings and cargo disgorged upon the island's coasts.

(September 7) Edward C. Bown wrote to the Department of Public Works (Halifax) reminding the Chairman of his letter and petition of the previous year, requesting the position as keeper on Scatarie Island. He called attention to his influential supporters, and mentioned getting further references from Jacob P. Miller, inspector of lighthouses.

Birth of Philip Sherwood Dodd, son of Philip Sherwood Dodd, Bridgeport merchant, and Susannah Weston (Haire) Dodd. Christening at St. George's Church, Sydney.

1836   Report in the *Journal and Proceedings of the House of Assembly of Nova Scotia* on the heroic rescue effected by James Dodd and his crew on Scatarie Island the preceding year:

". . . through the intrepidity and great activity of Mr. Dodd and his men, the whole Crew and Passengers, in all two hundred and seventy-four souls, of the Barque *William Ewing*, bound from Ireland to Quebec, and wrecked on the island, were safely landed, and have been forwarded to the place of their destination. The crews of two other vessels were also safely landed from wrecks. An expense of £80 16s 3d incurred."

"Ordered" (Saturday, March 12) "that Mr. Dodd [Edmund] have leave of absence from this House after Monday next to return home upon urgent private business."

(March) Mr. Stewart presented a bill to the House for the better regulation of Sable and Seal Islands.

Birth of Ellen Susannah Dodd, daughter of Philip Sherwood Dodd, Bridgeport merchant, and Susannah Weston (Haire) Dodd. Christening in St. George's Church, Sydney.

In the report of Lt. Col. Rice Jones, commanding the Royal Engineers: "Near the hill of the East Point of Scattarie [sic], about 20 or 30 feet above the level of the sea is considered to be the best site for a light House on that Island, and it is conveniently near to a little summer harbor for small craft, where materials can be most easily landed."

(March 12) Philip Dodd appointed Justice of the Peace for North-Eastern District of the County of Cape Breton.

Samuel Cunard and family travel (by boat) to Sydney to help celebrate the opening of a railway transporting coal from the mines to waiting ships.

(August 25) John Morrow, Consul of the United States in Nova Scotia, appointed Philip Dodd "my Consular agent in and for the Port of Sydney."

A bad year on Sable Island — more wrecks, less salvage and remuneration. New attention given the idea of building two lighthouses on the island.

1837 (February) "A Petition of Charles E. Leonard, Collector of the Colonial Revenue at Sydney, Cape Breton, was presented by Mr. Dodd and read, praying payment of certain expenses incurred by him in taking charge of and securing the Duties upon, the Cargoes of the Brig *Abeona,* wrecked on Scatarie Island. . . ."

Again a bill proposed in the House for the better regulation of Sable and Seal islands.

(February 23) ". . . the Hon. Samuel Cunard and Edmund M. Dodd, Esquire, to be Commissioners appointed on behalf of Lower Canada, New Brunswick and Prince Edward Island for the erection and maintenance of the Light-houses proposed to be built on the Islands of St. Paul and Scatarie."

Samuel Cunard and Edmund Dodd visit Scatarie for this purpose, and are paid £50 each for their trip.

"Bridgeport Mines are on the southern shore of Indian Bay. This establishment employs about 100 persons, the houses and buildings exceed 20 in number, exclusive of wharfs, sand pits, etc." (R.M.

Martin, *The British Colonial Library,* Vol. 41, 1837 (p. 109).

(July) A new petition recommending Edward C. Bown as keeper for the new lighthouse to be erected on Scatarie Island.

"Scatarie Island, for which vessels bound from England to our possessions in North America usually shape their course, lies a few miles from Mira Bay, on the south-east coast of Cape Breton. A light-house should for mere humanity sake be erected on this island, and I would entreat the attention of the patriotic brethern of the Trinity House, to the following facts obtained from a Halifax paper: — 'If we look to the comparative loss of life and property in these places, we shall not find that on Scatarie and St. Paul's to be trifling. The loss at the Isle of Sable, in the aggregate, during twenty-one years from 1806 to 1827 was about thirty-five vessels — two indeed of these were frigates, besides several ships and brigs; but a great part of them schooners and fishing vessels. In the vicinity of St. Paul's and Scatarie there have been in 1832, three ships, one barque, eight brigs and several small vessels, in all about 3,000 wrecked tons; and in 1833, four ships, four brigs and two schooners, near 2,800 tons and containing upward of 600 souls. How many more have suffered in these places, and at the Isle of Sable, who can tell. Here is a summary of the known loss in two years; but if the estimate be correct that the loss of shipping in the vicinity of St. Paul's and Scatarie, has been for the last twenty years about 2,000 tons per annum, how awfully great must be the loss from first to last, as in such cases in twenty years about 40,000 tons of shipping must have been wrecked in these two places, which is a far greater loss than at the Isle of Sable in the same given period. A recent calculation estimates the loss of life on these rocks during the past years at upwards of 1,000.' "

— Robert Montgomery Martin, *History of Nova Scotia,* 1837.

1838   (March 5) "A Bill to Incorporate a Company for the purpose of prosecuting the Whale Fishery by the name of the Nova Scotia Whaling Co."

Substantial whale bounties paid to Nova Scotia fishermen.

Cunard's steamships received a contract to deliver the mail. (His "ten gun brigs" had already been doing this job since 1833.)

Joseph Howe consulted Edmund Dodd, who had once fought a bloodless duel, about his own prospects for a duel he felt honor bound to participate in.

(June 11) John J. DeWolf, American Consul at Sydney appointed Philip Sherwood Dodd American Consular agent for Bridgeport.

1839   (January) A petition presented by Edmund M. Dodd requested aid for Sydney's Mechanics' Institute for establishing a library. (£20 granted in March).

(March 14) Death of Caroline Dodd (aged 2), daughter of Edmund Murray Dodd and Caroline Maria (Ritchie) Dodd.

(March 22) A bill for establishing a harbor master at Bridgeport (Agreed upon March 27 and 28).

(October 3) "The lighthouse recently erected on the north east end of Scaterie Island will be put into operation on the 1st of December next. The building is painted white and is elevated about 90' above sea level. A good boat will be kept there to go to the aid of boats in distress and a gun with which to answer signals." (*The Nova Scotian*).

1840   January 25 & 27 — A petition by Samuel Cunard for

whaling bounty (from the 1837 voyage of his company's ship *Rose*).

(May 22) Authorization from I.N. Bonar to Philip S. Dodd to collect light duties and excise duties.

Recommendation that "three Armed Cutters should be employed from the First day of April to the Middle of November, under the command of suitable persons, with a competent force for the protection of the Fishery and Revenue of this Province [Nova Scotia] — one to Cruise the Bay of Fundy, one from Cape Sable to Chedabucto Bay, and a third in the Gulf of St. Lawrence, and on the Coast of Cape-Breton."

1842   Drought in Sydney County . . . Swarms of grasshoppers . . . Hay failed.

"Desertion from the garrison [at Sydney] has become common."

(December 19) Hon. E.M. Dodd and Peter Hall Clarke, sureties, post $1,000 bond for Charles E. Leonard, to be appointed Collector of Provincial Duties.

E.M. Dodd judge of probate as well as Solicitor General (up to 1848).

1843   (January) Letter from C.E. Leonard, Collector of Duties, stating that since there has been a fast sailing boat patrolling the waters from Gabarus to Inganish [sic] he believes smuggling from St. Pierre & Miquelon, as well from Newfoundland, has decreased.

(February 17) "The committee have also had under consideration a letter to His Excellency, the Lieutenant-Governor from C.E. Leonard and others, Sydney, Cape Breton, on the expediency of erecting a Building at Sydney for the accommodation of Emigrants and Shipwrecked Mariners. The Committee are of the opinion that the recommendations contained therein are humane, and might occasionally be very convenient, but they do not feel justified in recommending a grant of money for that purpose for the present . . ."

Philip Dodd a J.P., along with Charles F. Leonard, Peter Hall Clarke and S.G. Archibald, all of whom signed a petition recommending payment of £28 10 6 for "relieving the misery of the crew of the *William Rippon.*"

Another petition on behalf of the Sydney Academy, read by Edmund M. Dodd.

The House concerned about the G.M.A. monopoly on Nova Scotia's mines.

Sable Island Establishment about to sell its schooner the *Sisters.*

(May 23) Birth of Murray Dodd, son of Edmund Murray Dodd and Caroline Maria (Ritchie) Dodd.

(May 24) Authorization from Rupert A. George (Provincial Secretary's office) to Philip Dodd (seizure officer in command of the government hired schooner) *Sylph* to 1) protect the fisheries 2) prevent smuggling.

E.M. Dodd told the House of Assembly that roads in Cape Breton were "so bad that travelling in a carriage was impractical."

1844   [August 6] Philip Dodd, seizing officer on the government schooner *Sylph*, directed the master to board an American fishing vessel, the *Argus* of Portland, Maine, which was fishing illegally (within the three mile limit) off Saint Ann's Bay, Cape Breton.

[August 19] Philip Dodd "now in charge of the Schooner *Sylph*, employed by the government of this province [Nova Scotia] for the protection of the trade of the province, and for the prevention of illicit trade."

[November 5] The *Argus* condemned as the result of a trial of her master William Doughty.

1845   (June 19) Birth of Marcus Dodd, son of Edmund M. Dodd and Caroline (Ritchie) Dodd. Married — July 15, Susan, only daughter of James R. Dodd, Scatarie, at Sherwood, Sydney by Rev. C. Inglis to Edward C. Bown. (*Novascotian*)

1847   (August 21) ". . . it has been whispered that Dodd [Edmund M.] will be seized, just before the assembling of Parliament, with a convenient attack of 'that' gout which has heretofore, on more occasions than once prevented his stirring from home." (*The Spectator*, Sydney)

(November 13) "The amount of shipping in the Harbor [Sydney] for the last few weeks has been greater than we almost ever remember it."

Birth of Rupert Davenport Dodd, son of Edmund M. Dodd and Caroline (Ritchie) Dodd.

A year of crop failure in Cape Breton.

1848   Joseph Howe, Hugh Bell, and the Receiver General of Nova Scotia conducted an inquiry into the conditions and past management at Sable Island.

E.M. Dodd made judge of the Supreme Court of Nova Scotia.

(December 17) Death of Philip Sherwood Dodd (Jr.) of Bridgeport, aged 13 years 8 months.

1849   (May 16) Death of Susannah (Gibbons) Dodd, aged 75.

1850   (September 6-14) Joseph Howe visited Sable Island to investigate complaints about mismanagement of the Establishment.

(October 21) Joseph Howe's report on conditions on Sable Island and his recommendations for improvements. Among the most significant of these were:

1) "The true position of the island ought to be determined, and accurate information circulated through all the communities trading on the Atlantic.

On the *Daring*'s cabin table lies the Chart by which she is navigated, published in 18--. Beside it lies a plan of the Island, including bearings and soundings, published by the late Superintendent [Darby] in 1824, and revised in 1829. Between these, discrepancies, frightful to contemplate, exist.

Captain Darby [of the *Daring*], by whom my attention was called to this topic, and who has had many years experience and great personal opportunities of comparison, believes his Father's plan to be correct. If so, and if the Charts in general use by the Navy and Mercantile Marine, are as inacurate as that which I found in the *Daring*, the errors will appear at a glance in this comparative statement . . . [see Report for Comparative latitudes].

The dangerous Bars beneath the sea, however carefully they may "have been examined in former times, appear to shift continually, and ought to be sounded within stated periods of five or ten years."

2) Recommended the building of a light house near the central station (thus disagreeing with Samuel Cunard, the senior commissioner of light houses, and Captain Darby, the commander of the cutter *Daring*). [See Report for Howe's numerous and convincing reasons for his stand on this matter.]

3) Advocated making Sable Island more productive. He judged that the island's potential for farming had not been sufficiently developed. Buildings for these farming operations could be constructed with lumber salvaged from wrecks. He recommended paying more attention to the breeding and upgrading of the island's horses so that 50 horses could be sold annually for from £15 to £20 each, instead of for the current 20 shillings to £5 apiece.

4) ". . . great care should be taken in selecting men for Sable Island. No hand should be shipped because employment was importunately demanded, or that an easy berth might be found for some person altogether unsuitable. Every man on the Island should be 'able bodied' in the full sense of the term. An athletic and fearless boat's crew it is indispensable to have. If the selections are made from among our hardy Shoremen, who combine fishing and farming, the best materials are ever at hand . . . ."

5) "No distinction is now made between the hands employed, for although Jackson performs the duty of second in command, he holds no rank as such, and gets no extra pay. A second officer should be appointed, wear a badge, and get £5 or £10 a year more than the rest. To this berth the men would aspire, and the hope of its possession would supply a motive to activity and good conduct."

1852   Philip S. Dodd commander of provincial schooner *Responsible* off the coast of Cape Breton and in the Gulf of Saint Lawrence. His letters during this year to his superiors Hugh Bell and Joseph Howe in Halifax were written chiefly from Port Hood.

[May 27] "Her majesty's ministers are desirous to remove all ground of complaint on the part of the colonies in consequence of the encroachment of the fishing vessels of the United States upon those waters, from which they are excluded by the terms of the convention of 1818, and they therefore intend to dispatch, as soon as possible, a small naval force of steamers, or other small vessels, to enforce the observance of that convention.

These vessels will, of course, be confined to the performance of the duties with which they are specially charged, and the commanders will be enjoined to exercise a careful discretion in the very delicate office of interfering with vessels belonging

to foreign and friendly powers."
[John S. Pakington]

[(June 23), Government House Halifax]

". . . On assuming the government, I found this provision made, and as the Season for preparation was short, I deemed it my duty, acting on the advice of the executive council, to give the necessary instructions for fitting out as many cutters as the sum voted would maintain.

These vessels were advertised for, prior to the receipt of Sir John Pakington's despatch of the 17th ultimo, announcing the determination of her majesty's government to employ an additional force of 'steamers, or other small vessels' on the coasts of North America this season.

Though this announcement was received with extreme satisfaction by the council, it was still thought desirable that the provincial cruizers should be fitted out and commissioned.

They are — the brigantines *Halifax* [commanded by James Laybold] and *Belle* [commanded by Paul Crowell], and the schooners *Daring* [commanded by James Daly] and *Responsible* [commanded by Philip Dodd]."

— John Bazalgette,
Administrator

[July 1] Cumberland at Halifax.

"Having . . . visited the three vessels, *Halifax, Belle,* and *Responsible*, which have been engaged by the colonial government, I consider it my duty to state my opinion of the insufficiency of their general equipment, when applied to control encroachment on the part of foreign fishing vessels said to be well fitted, and to be manned in many instances by a greater number of seamen than those engaged for the provincial vessels (15), which I consider about one half what is requisite; at present they are only equipped and manned as the merchant vessels employed on the coast, and were then armed with a few muskets — though it is proposed, as I understand, to procure a piece of ordinance for each vessel.

It is not unworthy to remark, that the crews of the American fishing vessels are frequently on shares, and that the crews of the protecting vessels, under the existing colonial law which assigns the penalty to the seizing officer, have not the personal interest in the seizure which the crews of the vessels encroaching have in defending their property.

I should therefore recommend that, as opportunities offer, means be taken to man the vessels more suitably for the important duties they have to perform, for if their present weakness should induce resistance, circumstances affecting the public honor and interest might occur, and the task of future protection by the vessels employed on the colonial service would be rendered more difficult."

— G.F. Seymour
Vice admiral and commander in chief.

[July 8] "The fishing vessels of the United States are found in great numbers at Port Hood and adjacent harbors in Cape Breton, New Brunswick, and those of Prince Edward Island, where they pass their Sundays, and the men land in great numbers, which leads to illegal traffic, and to an undue influence over the inhabitants, and from their numbers are beyond control."

— from a "Memorandum of legal questions relating to the North American fisheries" by G.F. Seymour, Vice admiral and commander-in-chief.

[September 2] Excerpts from a "Memorial" signed by many Merchants and Inhabitants of Halifax and other parts of Nova Scotia protesting British laxness in protecting the N.S. fisheries: "By the mail recently arrived from England, your memorialists have learned, with deep concern, that it is in contemplation of your majesty's ministers to surrender to the United States of America privileges of fishing on the

137

coasts of your majesty's North American colonies, to which, at present, your majesty's subjects are alone entitled."

* * *

[November 10] HMSS *Devastation,* Halifax: "During July, when the mackarel [sic] strike in, the Americans arrive in their very fine schooners in pursuit of them. The fish are only to be taken close along shore, so that if they do not encroach they must be unsuccessful . . . . in fine weather, you cannot run the North Shore down without seeing 100 United States fishery vessels, sometimes 150, which carry, on an average, 500 barrels, worth, say at least £2 sterling per barrel; supposing that only 100 vessels fill up once.

It seems to be a clearly established fact, that not only is the mackerel valuable in itself, but, where that fish is plentiful, the cod is also so.

* * *

" . . . I have no hesitation in stating my belief that, with 12 boats well manned and in charge of officers possessing energy and zeal, the Americans might be kept entirely off all the fishing grounds of that part of the Gulf on which the *Devastation* was lately stationed."
— Colin Yorke Campbell, commander
[November 30] Halifax.

* * *

"In conclusion, I would respectfully call the attention of the Government: 1st, to the loose manner in which the business of entering and clearing vessels is carried on about the Island of Cape Breton, by some of the provincial officers; and 2nd, to a practice which I believe prevails to a large extent in the neighborhood of Canso, Cape Breton and P. E. Island; American fishing vessels are fitted out and supplied in their own ports, clear out

138

and sail for the fishing grounds around our shores, enter our ports, where they are transferred to British subjects, who obtain registers for them, under which they fish and sail throughout the season; when the fishing is done they return as American Vessels to the American port from whence they first sailed . . . ."

— from letter of Captain James Laybold of the *Halifax* to Joseph Howe

[January 14] Halifax

"In fact the American fishermen have the sole control of the Strait of Canso, and do whatever they please. When their vessels have been boarded by me, although courteous and ready in their answers, they still show a great reluctance to move off when requested . . . .

* * *

The American fishermen deserve a great deal of praise. Their vessels are of the very best description, beautifully rigged, and sail remarkably fast; well found in every particular, and carry large crews, a great many of whom are men from the provinces. The difference between the American and English vessels is very great, for of all the English vessels in the Gulf of St. Lawrence the past fall, there were only four or five could in any way compete with the American . . . .

* * *

The coast affording such poor shelter, Port Hood is the general rendezvous; as many as 250 sail have been at times at anchor there, and from the middle of October all vessels endeavor to get in before dark — American as well as English — which is a great complaint amongst our fishermen.

* * *

The mackerel fishery about Sable Island has

this year failed. The fishery is done with small boats, close to the shore, and principally close to the north west bar. The weather has been very tempestuous about the island, as well as on the shores of this province, and consequently the sea has been too rough for fishing.

* * *

In explanation of the words, various duties, used at the beginning of this report, I beg leave to state, that the *Daring* has been employed during the season, in taking provisions to Canso, for the relief of the poor of Guysborough county; taking the members of the provincial parliament to Arichat, Gut of Canso, and Guysborough; taking the judge to Sydney; taking oil and light house stores to all the light houses in the Bay of Fundy . . .; taking the mail and passengers to Newfoundland; visiting Sable Island nine times, and bringing therefrom the materials of schooner *Star-of-Hope*, wrecked on that Island in December, 1851, bringing the crew and materials of American fishing schooner *Navara,* wrecked on the island in September of the past year; and in bringing the crew and part of cargo and materials of brigt. *Ottoman,* of St. John's, Newfoundland, wrecked on the island in November last."

— from Report of Captain James Daly
of the *Daring*

1853   (May 16) In a letter to Hugh Bell, Chairman of the Department of Public Works, Halifax, M.D. McKenna, then Superintendeant of Sable Island wrote: ". . . Brady the carpenter has been very insolent and provoked me to strike him this morning . . . Brady refused to stop a team that was moving in my direction when I called to him to do so the Teamster being absent . . . And when I told him to take his hands out of his pockets and do his work he told me that I was not able to make him do otherwise

140

nor was any man on the Island able to do it when I instantly with foot and fist convinced him that he had made a mistake when he took my dimensions . . . ."

Final removal of the garrison from Sydney.

(July 24) Boat sailed for Sable Island with orders to take off 100 horses.

Publication of British Admiralty chart of Sable Island.

Miss Dix visited Sable Island, and, subsequently had 3 excellent lifeboats sent to the Humane Establishment as well as a library of 300 books.

1854   (January 1) Death of Archibald Otto Dodd (aged 24), son of Edmund M. Dodd and Mary Ann Sarah (Weeks) Dodd, murdered by the father of a girl he supposedly raped.

M.D. McKenna wrote from Sable Island to complain of the bad state of repair of the *Daring*, a vessel which he noted was then ten years old and had never had any repairs.

1855   (February 10) Death of James Richard (Raymond) Dodd: "Midshipman James Raymond Dodd, son of Chief Justice Dodd, served in many actions and left the Royal Navy after the American War of 1812, served as lighthouse keeper at Scatarie Island after 1838 and died at Sydney February 10, 1855. (*Acadian Recorder*, February 24)

February 17 — "Under our obituary heading today appears a notice of the death of James R. Dodd, Esq., the late Superintendent of Scatarie Lighthouse, and of the Humane Establishment there — the trying and responsible duties appertaining to which appointments he faithfully and zealously discharged for many years . . . . In the deceased the shipwrecked mariner and emigrant

found a generous and tender hearted friend, and few who enjoyed his acquaintance but have shared in his hospitalities and kindness. To the fishermen who located themselves on Scatarie Island during the fishing season, he was particularly kind — acting towards the sick both as a physician and a friend."
Cape Breton News)

Edmund J. Dodd appointed superintendent of Scatarie.

(August 8) A letter sent to Miss Dix from the secretary of the Royal Benevolent Society, London, England related to the exceptional services of Captain McKenna at Sable Island (in connection with saving the crew and passengers of the *Arcadia* and other vessels wrecked on the island) and informing her that a gold medal had been awarded to Captain McKenna.

(September) Philip Dodd appointed superintendent of Sable Island, replacing M.D. McKenna.

Mrs. Howard whose husband kept the Parrsboro light asked, upon his death, if she could take his place. Mr. Bell, Chairman of the Board of Works, replied that her request could not be considered as "there is no lighthouse in charge of a female."

1856   Philip Dodd experienced a good many difficulties on Sable Island. Among the most distressing was a quarrel with his predecessor, M.D. McKenna.

1857   (September 14) A letter from Philip Dodd on Sable Island to the Halifax authorities regarding authorization for a mining company to prospect on Sable.

(September 27) Approval from the Provincial Secretary's Office to look for natural mineral deposits on Sable Island. Stipulations that exploration be limited to four workmen at any one time. Workers are to be subject to the authority of the Board of Trade and the superintendent of the island.

1858   (September 29) Authorization for mining on Sable Island.

1859   Death of Reverend William Young Porter of Sydney by drowning after falling through the ice in Sydney Harbor. "He left behind a widow and seven children destitute."

Rebuilding of St. George's in Sydney with stone from Louisbourg.

1861   (March) Edward Bown, lightkeeper at Devil's Island, dismissed.

(June 1) Edmund S. Dodd resigned as Superintendent of Scatarie Island. John McLean appointed in his stead.

1862   (February 24) M.D. McKenna wrote to Hugh Munro, Chairman of the Board of Works recommending the introduction of Albertine Oil [Kerosene] at some of Nova Scotia's lighthouses. He was convinced that it would provide stronger, cleaner, less expensive light than seal oil. He suggested trying Albertine Oil, in the Devil's Island light and one other, pointing out that it had been used at the Maugher's Beach light in the summer of 1851 and elicited a favorable response.

(March 20) Death of Edmund S. Dodd (aged 27).

M.D. McKenna recommended the use of Albertine oil instead of sperm oil at Scatarie Island, together with a reduced number (from 3 to 2) of men at the Establishment.

(November 27) Licence to J.A. Philipps and John Darlington of London Mining Engineers to search for minerals at Sable Island.

1863   (March 10) "Richard Collier Bernard Marshall DesBarres Gibbons (Susannah Gibbons Dodd's brother) died at his residence near Sydney . . . in the 84th year of his age."

Publication of the revised edition of the 1853 British Admiralty chart of Sable Island.

1864   Matthew D. McKenna appointed officer for protection of the revenue throughout the province [Nova Scotia].

1865   Philip S. Dodd made a Notary Public.

(May 2) Murray Dodd called to the bar of Nova Scotia, and at once entered the practice of his profession in Sydney.

". . . the decease of Edmund Murray Dodd, Esq., eldest surviving son of the Hon. Mr. Justice Dodd, who departed this life at 7 o'clock on Monday evening last, at the early age of 27 years. For several years past the deceased resided at Lingan, where he filled the offices of Collector of Customs, and Consular Agent for the United States; but owing to the delicate state of his health, he had, during the present winter, removed to Town, and made his father's house his home. No immediate fatal results, however, were apprehended; hence the unexpected announcement of his death caused universal grief throughout this community. Here, and elsewhere, he was generally beloved and esteemed; nor could it be otherwise. Possessed of tender sensibilities, of an amiable disposition, and a manly heart, he had won for himself the regard and affection of all. At home he was the particular object of parental love and solicitude . . ."

1866   Marcus Dodd (aged 21) graduated in medicine from
              the College of Physicians and Surgeons, New York,
              and returned to Cape Breton to practise at the
              International Mines, Bridgeport.

1867   (July 1) Confederation. The Sable Island Humane
              Establishment now administered by the federal
              government.

              (October 1) Murray Dodd appointed registrar of the
              court of probate for the county of Cape Breton (an
              office he held until 1872).

              (December 13) Burial of Charles William
              Macarmick Dodd, eldest son of A.C. Dodd and
              half-pay officer in Sydney. Aged 77.

1869   (April 27) M.C. McKenna appointed Justice of the
              Peace in Shelbourne County.

              (May 7) Death of Charles E. Leonard aged 86.

1871   Cotton Mather Almon (Elley Dodd's husband and
              Philip Sherwood Dodd's son-in-law) "contested the
              county of Stagatag, Manitoba in the Liberal-
              Conservative interest and was defeated by a
              Frenchman by a small majority . . . ."

1872   Murray Dodd appointed judge of the probate for
              Cape Breton.

1873   Dr. Marcus Dodd married Sarah C. Rigby. Her
              brother Charles had been manager of the Glace Bay
              Mining Association.

              Philip Dodd's return from Sable Island.

1875   (October 31) Death of Rupert Davenport Dodd
              (aged 28), son of E.M. Dodd and Maria Ritchie
              Dodd.

1876   (April 9) Death of Susannah Weston (Haire) Dodd, aged 66.

1882   (Dec. 2) Death of Philip Sherwood Dodd, aged 76.

Appendix B

List of Cape Breton's Governors:

1784-1787	Colonel Joseph Frederick Wallet DesBarres
1787-1795	Lieutenant Colonel Macarmick
1795-1798	David Matthews
1798-1799	Brigadier-General Ogilvie
1799-1800	Brigadier-General Murray
1800-1807	Major-General Despard
1807-1813	Brigadier-General Nepean
1813-1816	Brigadier-General Swayne
1816 (February 5 to November 4)	Lieutenant-Colonel Fitzherbert
1816-1820	Major-General Ainslie

Appendix C

Copy of Entries in Family Bible
of Archibald Charles Dodd

Children of Archibald Charles Dodd and Susannah Gibbons, married 8 July, 1788.

1. **Charles William Macarmick Dodd** born 20 August, 1790 at 1/4 past five in the morning, was Christened by the Revd. Mr. Cossit. Sponsors, William Macarmick Governor of Cape Breton.
William Cox Captain 21st. Regiment and Mrs. Cox. Small pox by Innoculation 15 Feb. 1808. Hooping Cough 1796. Mumps 1809.

2. **Susannah Helen Dodd** born 14 December 1793 about 10 o'clock in the morning. Baptised. Innoculated at Halifax 1800. Variole. Hooping Cough 1796.

3. **James Richard Dodd** born 13 December, 1795, 1/2 past 11 o'clock at night. Baptised. Sponsors James Remon Esqr. Isld of Jersey. Richard Stout Esqr., Sydney, C. Breton. Innoculated 23 Feb. 1801. Hooping Cough 1796. Mumps and Measles at Halifax, 1803.

4. **Edmund Mathews Murray** born 9 January 1797 1/4 past

12 o'clock Noon. Christened. Sponsors Wm. Despard, nephew of General Despard, David Mathews, Esqr. Son of the late Attorney General. Mrs. Murray, widow. Innoculated 23 Feb. 1801. Hooping Cough 1802. Measles and Mumps at Halifax, 1809.

5. **Anna Kearney Caroline Dodd** born 14 June, 1799 1/4 past 4 a.m. Christened. Sponsors Francis Kearney, Lt. Colonel N.S. Regiment. Anna Kearney his Lady and Susannah Gibbons Mother of Mrs. Dodd. Innoculated Feb. 1801. Hooping Cough 1802. Mumps 1809.

6. **John Despard Dodd** born 28 September 1801 at 1/4 past 2 a.m. Monday. Christened. Sponsors Major General John Despard, Francis Hearney, Lt. Col. N. Scotia Rt., Mrs. Despard, the General's Lady. Vaccinated 1804. Hooping Cough 1802. Mumps 1809.

7. **Caroline Dorothy Louisa Arrow** born 14 January 1804 at 10 p.m. Saturday. Christened. Sponsors Richard Gibbons Esqr. brother to Mrs. Dodd. Mrs. Dumaresq wife of the Collector of the Customs. Miss Dorothy Cox, daughter of Captain Cox. Vaccinated 1804 Mumps 1809. Hooping Cough 1811.

8. **Philip Sherwood Dodd** born Wednesday 16 July 1806, 2 o'clock a.m. Baptised. Sponsors. Vacinated at Halifax 1808. Mumps at the same time. Hooping cough 1811.

9. **Bertha Dodd** born 28 April, 1809, 8 o'clock a.m. Baptised. Sponsors. Vaccinated 1810. Hooping Cough 1811.

10. **Julia Adelaide** born 8 November 1811 at half past 5 o'clock a.m. Christened. Sponsors, Major General Nepean, Miss Susanna Dodd, Mrs. Mary Clarke.

11. **Ellen Amelia Dodd** born on Saturday the 15th day of October, 1814 at 1/4 before 5 o'clock a.m.

Appendix D

Philip Dodd's View of the Fisheries Disputes

The "Argus" affair

"I have the honor to acknowledge the receipt of your letter of the 13 instant with an extract of a Dispatch received by His Excellency the Lieutenant Governor from her Majesty's Principal Secretary of State for the Colonies having reference to a charge against me as late commander of the Revenue Schooner *Sylph* for harsh treatment to the Master and Crew of the American fishing vessel *Argus* seized by me, on the occasion in question. In reply I have to state for the information of His Excellency the Lieutenant Governor that when in command of the *Sylph* on the Sixth of August last when cruising round the Coast of Cape Breton, I discovered the *Argus* actually employed fishing and altho more than three miles from any land still much within the Bay that is formed by a straight line drawn from Cape North to the Northern Head of Cow Bay, and consequently I felt it my duty to take her into Sydney being the nearest Port to me at the time at which an officer of Her Majesty's Customs was stationed . . .

After the gross misrepresentation of Doughty master of the *Argus*, every line of his affidavit being

150

marked with falsehood, it would almost induce me should I again be honored with the command of one of the Provincial Revenue Vessels not to go out of my way for the mere purpose of extending to the class of persons to which Mr. Doughty belongs those acts of kindness and courtesy with which he was favoured but which have been returned by the blackest ingratitude . . . ."

— portions of a letter from Philip Dodd,
written at Sydney, December 23, 1844

At the time, Philip had found the *Argus* affair unsettling. He had been upset by the charges that he had mistreated her master and crew. In retrospect, however, Philip had long since realized that the confrontation which his seizure of this vessel had provoked had been almost worth the trouble. Once the difficulties had been resolved, patrolling certain stretches of Nova Scotia's coast had been a little less frustrating.

* * *

It had been because of the fog that he had caught Doughty and his crew red-handed. Ordinarily, in clear weather, the *Sylph* was recognizable from so great a distance that captains of American vessels fishing illegally in Nova Scotian waters had plenty of time to act innocent and to destroy the evidence. But that early August day, Philip had happened upon the *Argus* so suddenly that there had been no opportunity for crew and captain to disguise their activities.

Indeed, the fog had been so dense that Philip and his men had been unaware of a second vessel, a sister craft, fishing alongside the *Argus* at the time she had been taken into custody. It was only when this second fishing schooner had followed them into Sydney in order to offer Doughty support that he had realized that she had been within earshot of the whole proceedings, though hidden within the fog bank.

The three schooners had arrived in Sydney the morning of the 7th of August. In accordance with his instructions for dealing with such cases, Philip had at once handed over the *Argus* and her crew to the collector of customs, Mr. Davenport. The latter, an old family friend, had agreed with Philip's suggestion that the master and crew of the seized vessel be allowed to remain on board thirty hours after dropping anchor in Sydney Harbor. This would give them ample time to collect their private property.

However, at the end of this allotted period, Captain Doughty had asked for an extension, and Philip, ready to oblige, had accompanied the *Argus*'s master to Davenport's office. But the inspector of customs, though a fair and reasonable man, had refused to let Doughty and his crew stay on board their vessel any longer.

Davenport had stated that, since he was now personally responsible for the *Argus*'s inventory, he could not risk a repetition of what had happened in 1838 aboard the *Hero* of Eastport. The crew of this vessel, which had been seized under circumstances similar to those governing the taking of the *Argus*, had also been billeted on board, and they had systematically stripped their vessel of everything moveable. Davenport had been, he reminded Philip, personally accountable for the loss.

Besides, Davenport had been concerned that Doughty and his crew, with the assistance of the master and crew of the *Argus*'s sister vessel, might, once the *Sylph* had returned to sea, attempt to recapture their schooner. He had fretted about this a good deal because, on the afternoon of the day the *Argus* had been brought into Sydney Harbor, he had come upon two seamen on the street complaining loudly to another gentleman about the harshness with which the crew of the *Sylph* had treated the crew of the *Argus*. One of these men had been the master of the *Argus*'s sister craft.

Yet when Davenport had suggested that this man file an official complaint he had not done so. And a day and a half later, when Doughty had been told that he and his crew would have to vacate the *Argus*, no one had made any fuss. Doughty, Davenport, the American Consul and Philip himself had settled the matter amicably — or so it had seemed. In fact, the whole affair had appeared cut and dried. Doughty and his crew had not had a leg to stand on, and they had seemed to accept the inevitable loss of their vessel. Doughty had even thanked Philip for his gentlemanly conduct in allowing himself and his men time to collect their personal belongings, and for his kindness in providing them with a passage as far as Halifax on board the *Sylph*.

Then, in early November when the trial was held, the owners of the *Argus* had allowed their vessel to be condemned in the Admiralty Court in Halifax without putting forward any defence whatsoever. It had appeared that the matter was finally closed, that the Americans had accepted the penalty for being caught in their violation of the 1818 treaty.

So Doughty's complaint that he, Philip, had mistreated him and his crew, had come out of the blue. Accompanied by affidavits from members of the *Argus*'s crew, these accusations had for a while even been taken seriously. Philip's superiors in Halifax had put him on the spot so that he, in turn, had had to collect affidavits to substantiate his own report of what had taken place.

Fortunately, this had been no problem. Davenport had come forward with a detailed account which had mirrored his own, and several of his crew had also given sworn statements to back him up. He had even been ready to enlist the support of the American consul when the whole proceeding had been dropped.

Yet despite his exoneration, Philip had brooded over Doughty's unexpectedly underhanded behavior . . . the unfairness of his accusations. It had all come as such a surprise, since, at the time of the arrest, there had been no face to face confrontation between himself and Doughty — or between Doughty and Davenport either. Everything had been conducted in a proper and gentlemanly manner. On leaving the *Sylph* in Halifax, Doughty had even shaken hands with him and thanked him for his consideration. It had seemed unthinkable that the same man could suddenly, a few months later, do such an about face . . . turn on him with a whole pack of lies. This was what had rankled. Philip had resolved that he would, in future, be less considerate of American fishermen of what he considered to be Doughty's type.

* * *

Reinstated on the *Sylph* as seizing officer the following season, Philip found that the *Argus* affair had set him thinking more seriously about the presence of American fishermen in Nova Scotia's coastal waters. He had assumed a more aggressive attitude which had been apparent in several suggestions he had made in his report for the year 1845.

The most significant of these recommendations as far as his own future was concerned — and indeed the only one his superiors had attended to — had had to do with the relative uselessness of the schooner *Sylph* in apprehending Americans fishing within the limits. The distinctive contours of her hull and rigging, Philip had pointed out, at once alerted the foreign fishermen to the presence of the government cruiser. Even at a great distance she was clearly recognizable. If, instead of the *Sylph*, Philip had suggested, a fore and aft schooner or shallop — a vessel which resembled the New Englanders' own craft — was used, the intruders would perhaps be less venturesome and the fisheries' officers were successful in apprehending them.

The success of this idea had been proved the following season when the *Argus* had replaced the *Sylph* on coastal patrols and Philip had been appointed seizing officer on the former American vessel. That year and the following year as well, he had successfully boarded and charged masters of American fishing vessels from the Tusket Islands to Cape Breton.

His missions had, he guessed, been least useful in the vicinity of Port Hood where the American vessels congregated in large numbers and where the local inhabitants invariably supported the intruders, even to the extent of forewarning them when they knew that the revenue cutters were in the vicinity.

Such had been the case in early October 1847 when Philip, meeting up by chance with Captain Darby* of the *Daring* in a cove near the Gut of Canso, had rigged up a plan

---

* James Darby was the son of Joseph Darby, superintendent of the Sable Island Humane Establishment from 1830 to 1848. He died off Sable Island on the *Daring* toward the end of Matthew McKenna's superintendency, and McKenna was obliged to sail the *Daring* back to Halifax.

154

for the two vessels to return to Port Hood together. Singly neither government schooner could hope to take the Americans, but together they had a chance.

However, word of their coming had preceded them. Four men in a boat from Port Hood had reached the American fishing fleet first and warned them of the coming of the two revenue cutters. The Americans had promptly weighed anchor and set sail for home, their fishing over for the season.

Philip would never have known how the American fleet had got wind of their coming, if an American captain had not boarded the *Argus* and told his crew while he had been off in the small boat .... A strange business however you looked at it!

Crosscurrents: from the bridge
of the *Responsible*, 1852

"On Friday last I had the honor of seeing the admiral on board HMS *Basilisk*, off Port Hood Island, and received from him a copy of two statements made by American fishermen, with reference to information said to have been given by me.

1st. R.W. Armstead, master of U.S. schr. *Angenora*, of Frankfort states that, about the 27th of July last, he went on board the schr. *Responsible*, and was informed by her commander, that if he found him fishing within three marine miles of a line drawn from Cape Gaspé to the north point of Prince Edward Island, he would seize his vessel.

2nd. William Page, master of U.S. schr. *Paragon*, of Newburyport, stated to Mr. Sutton, that, on or about the 23rd day of July, he was informed by the commander of the schr. *Responsible,* that he would draw a line from headland to headland on any part of the coast of Nova Scotia, and seize any vessel he found fishing within three miles of such a line.

These statements I have copied verbatim, and although not called upon to answer them, I still think it my duty to do so. The first is altogether false; there has not been any American captain on board the schr. *Responsible* since I have had charge of her, except a captain Dixon, of the schooner *Empire* which vessel was repairing at that time in the Strait of Canso; and again, on the twenty-seventh of July, the schr. *Responsible* was coming up from Margaree Island, both which facts can be attested to if required by half the ship's company . . . .

The assertion of William Page, master of the schooner *Paragon*, may be correct, for I did to several American captains . . . say, that I should draw a line from the headlands of the coast and bays of Cape Breton, and seize all American vessels found trespassing within three marine miles of such line; and such are my intentions until further orders, as I consider myself bound to do so by my instructions, in which I am referred to the convention of 1818 . . . and also by the result of the trial of the American schooner *Argus*, which vessel was seized by me . . . and condemned . . . ."

— from a letter written by Philip Dodd to the Provincial Secretary, Joseph Howe, from Port Hood, August 29, 1852.

The aggressiveness of American fishermen in Nova Scotian waters, which Philip thought had eased somewhat about the time the *Argus* had replaced the *Sylph* in 1846, had become worse than ever by 1851. It was clear that the Americans had become more brazen. They largely ignored the conditions of the treaty of 1818. To fish illegally they took more risks and engaged in more sophisticated frauds than previously.

To combat this growing American lawlessness — and what looked remarkably like a New England takeover of the best Nova Scotian fisheries — dramatic steps had to be taken. And so, at the beginning of the 1852 season, the provincial government had commissioned four vessels to share the job of patrolling coastal waters — the brigantines, *Halifax* and *Belle* and the schooners, *Daring* and *Responsible*.

The *Daring* had, of course, already been in the government service for a good many years, and had been used as a revenue cutter before. Captain Darby, her master when Philip had been seizing officer on the *Sylph* and the *Argus*, had worked with him on more than one occasion to catch American vessels breaking the treaty. James Daly, another good man, had been given command of the *Daring* after

Darby's sudden death off Sable Island. Still the effectiveness of the *Daring* as a fisheries and revenue cruiser had always been limited by all the other demands made on her time — by her numerous runs to Sable Island, by her transporting of cargo and personnel to this and other Humane Establishments as well as to lighthouses from Cape Breton to the Bay of Fundy, by her excursions with governor or bishop to Sydney, Shelburne, Yarmouth or Digby . . . .

Yet the manoeuvers of the *Daring* and the *Responsible*, the *Halifax* and the *Belle*, together with Commander Colin Campbell's charge, the *Devastation*, and the admiral's vessel, the *Basilisk*, had seemed for a while on the verge of discouraging the Americans.

* * *

At the beginning of the 1852 fall season there had been more American fishing vessels passing through the Gut of Canso and congregating close to shore in the choice grounds between Port Hood and Margaree Islands than Philip had ever seen. There were, continuously, close to a hundred sail* off each island. At night all would anchor in the lee of these islands, weighing next morning (if no fisheries patrol vessel were nearby), throwing their bait over and drifting off shore.

By such leisurely fishing each vessel soon had a full fare; and, at the height of the season, American captains would frequently make two or three trips each to these superb and tranquil fishing grounds. There was here, they found, as good a take as on the banks off Sable Island or Newfoundland, with few of the risks involved in frequenting the foggy and turbulent North Atlantic off these remote coasts. (Besides, by autumn, word had got around that the fisheries off Sable had failed that season, the weather having been too inclement.)

Yet over and above all the natural advantages of fishing off Port Hood and Margaree, was the friendliness of the inhabitants. On the nearby shore were those who would provide the New Englanders with bait, buy goods they had

---

* This expression (in the singular) was used widely during the era of sailing vessels.

157

brought along to trade, socialize when the weather was too bad to fish, sign on if vessels were shorthanded, give warnings of the approach of government vessels, and even furnish false Colonial papers.

It was in the end the collusion of the local people which had defeated Philip and his fellow officers. Despite the advantages the American captains had — superior vessels, greater capital backing them, a "half-hand" share system whereby each man got half his own catch — by late in the 1852 season, it had become apparent that continuous and determined harassment by the *Devastation*, the *Responsible* and other government vessels, had all but routed the Americans. By mid-October most of the Americans had weighed anchor and sailed for home — a good month earlier than usual.

Yet everyone surmised that next season the New Englanders would be back in full force, having taken more care to secure fake identity papers. They had learned that if they were clever enough in falsifying their vessels' documents, detection and acquiring proof of fraudulence was a difficult and time-consuming business for the boarding officers. Indeed, the lesson which Her Majesty's officers had learned was that they had to be absolutely sure of the American vessels being at fault before pressing charges. And even then they needed sufficient witnesses since the American masters — mostly so polite face to face — were in the habit of filing official complaints later. All too many behaved like Doughty of the *Argus*.

They lied about their papers, the fish they had caught, the location where they had been apprehended . . . . And then, a good many had had the audacity to complain to the Nova Scotia authorities that *they* had been harassed and unfairly treated by the seizing officers of the revenue vessels. Some even claimed compensation.

As the 1852 season had progressed it had seemed to Philip that the commanders of the government vessels — *not* the captains of the American fishing schooners — were being harassed . . . and by their own government. While on one hand the provincial authorities had to appear to be trying to safeguard Nova Scotia's fisheries, on the other, it seemed that

158

the officials in Halifax — Joe Howe amongst them — were increasingly leery of provoking the New Englanders.

Philip could see why in retrospect. If there had been an out and out confrontation — a show of force — there was little doubt that the Americans would have had the upper hand.

Nevertheless, Philip, Laybold, Daly, Crowell and Campbell had been placed in impossible situations — operating with a supposed mandate to arrest offenders, and yet, as the season progressed, receiving more and more instructions to move carefully, to avoid confrontations.

They had all — some more than others — been sucked into the crosscurrents. Totally uncharted, such political turbulence was for mariners like themselves more dangerous than the notorious but well-known crosscurrents around the Tuskets or Sable Island.

Philip himself and Daly too had not been pulled in so deeply as the others. They had learned to be somewhat wary where politicians were concerned. Consequently, they had, as much as possible, operated at the edge of the maelstrom. Philip had preferred to avoid another confrontation comparable to the *Argus* affair; and Daly, even after a short stint as master of the *Daring* had, apparently, realized how closely accountable he was to the House for all his actions on board the government schooner and had crimped his style accordingly.

Yet in that memorable 1852 season even Daly had had a number of unpleasant skirmishes with American captains — conflicts which had only just stopped short of arrests. The most disagreeable of these had, according to Daly, been his boarding of the schooner *Leonard McKenzie* of Gloucester, a larger, faster vessel than the *Daring*, and commanded by a Shelburne man named Demins. The *Daring* had come up to the *Leonard McKenzie* which had been anchored off Port Hood, and Daly had boarded the American vessel only to find that her lines were all wet but the hooks cut off. The crew, Daly said, had been so abusive that they had threatened either to heave him overboard or take him back to the United States. However, after taking the *Leonard MacKenzie* into Port Hood and searching the schooner from stem to stern, Daly and his men had, so they said, not found sufficient cause to detain the vessel.

Paul Crowell had been involved in a similar incident —
with a somewhat different outcome — off Pubnico in July. The
Belle had come upon an American schooner, the *Helen
Maria* of Gloucester, apparently fishing mackerel between
Argyle and John's Island.

Crowell, upon boarding the American schooner, and
finding mackerel obviously taken that day, had placed the
vessel under arrest and accompanied her to Pubnico. Mr.
Willet and Mr. d'Entremont at the customs house there had
agreed with Crowell and his men that the fish on board the
Helen Maria had clearly been caught that day — a judgement
substantiated by a fisherman of Argyle who had actually seen
the crew of the American vessel taking the mackerel at Argyle
(and within the three mile limit).

The case had seemed cut and dried, yet Crowell, just to
make sure that he would find backing for his actions in the
Provincial Secretary's Office, had telegraphed Howe. The brief
reply, which, by the summer's end, all the commanders of the
government cruisers had memorized, had come back in
writing: "There being reason to hope that friendly negotiation
may, before long, adjust the fishery question, his excellency the
lieutenant governor is unwilling to press upon Captain Spin-
ney [of the *Helen Maria*] in the meantime, a severe construction of the law; I have therefore been commanded to authorize
you to release the *Helen Maria.*"

Written that same day [August 6] was another letter
[one which Philip had just come across again in going through
his papers]. It too had been addressed to Crowell, but Howe
had directed that a copy be sent as well as Laybold, Daly and
Philip himself, warning them to be careful about making
arrests: ". . . in view of the risks which may follow any
indiscretion on the part of the officers commanding the
provincial cruisers, his excellency will hold them strictly
accountable for any want of prudence . . . ." Campbell of the
Devastation had not been sent one of these letters, and it had
almost proved his undoing.

Philip remembered all the hours he had spent
pondering this ambiguous message. Was one supposed to do
one's job or not? Daly and Laybold, he later found out, had
felt the same way. It had certainly seemed as if, despite their

original orders, they were meant to turn a blind eye to American infringements of the 1818 convention.

They had all attempted to follow Howe's somewhat nebulous instructions — and had pretty much done so until late September when Laybold of the *Halifax* had boarded the *Meridian* at Port Hood and taken her in. The *Meridian* had on board two masters — an American, Joshua Dodge, and a British subject, John Williams. Suspicious circumstances indeed!

Despite Dodge's and Williams' assertions that the *Meridian* had recently been transferred from American to British registry, Laybold had remained dubious — and had pressed for an investigation. After all, when he had boarded the *Meridian* earlier in the month at Canso, she had had American papers only!

Laybold's suspicions had proved well-founded. The *Meridian*, while possessing new British papers, acquired at Canso, had still been on the books in Castine, Maine. The transfer of registry had been a pretense. This kind of fraud, Laybold had protested in his year-end report, was, as far as he could judge, widespread: the *Meridian* hoax had not been an isolated instance.

Despite the mounting evidence against the American master, there had been no quick trial and conviction as there had been during the *Argus* affair. Times had changed.

Just how much they had changed had been demonstrated by the official reaction to Colin Campbell's overzealous carrying out of his orders. Placing political concerns aside, he had made arrests — dozens of them — at Margaree, at Port Hood, and elsewhere. He had not only boarded American vessels like the *Creole*, charging their masters with illegal practices, but he had also boarded and charged captains of dozens of colonial vessels.

A number of these cases had subsequently been tried and dismissed in the Admiralty Court. Protests and petitions for compensation from owners from New England to Lunenburg had then flooded in; and, because the charges had not stuck, Campbell, in an odd turn of events, had for a while been held responsible for paying a portion of the costs of the trials, together with compensation for fishing time lost.

The wrangling had gone on throughout the following year — particularly over the *Creole*, which, though freed, had, as several members of the House pointed out, been in the wrong. By 1854 House members were still arguing the pros and cons. Campbell's position, as Philip and everyone else could see, was an impossible one. This had seemed a good time to get off the fisheries and revenue cutters.

Appendix E

The first five superintendents of the Sable Island Humane Establishment:

1801-1809   James Morris

1809-1830   Edward Hodgson

1830-1848   Joseph Darby

1848-1855   Matthew D. McKenna

1855-1873   Philip Dodd

Appendix F

The following is a partial list of vessels which foundered on or near Scatarie Island between 1831 and 1855, together with particulars concerning them. The source of the majority of these entries was the *Journals and Proceedings of the House of Assembly of Nova Scotia* and Cape Breton newspapers of the period; and all quotations, unless otherwise identified, are from these records. Other sources were *The Blue Book* of Statistics pertaining to Nova Scotia and various newspapers and petitions in the Public Archives of Nova Scotia.

1831   All aboard the brig *Ceres*, were "cast away on the island of Scatarie . . . . The master and crew were much frost-bitten and in distress."

1832   (August 11 or 12) The *Leonidas*, a transport vessel "conveying troops and a large amount of specie to the military chest in Canada was wrecked on the Island of Scatari [sic] and totally lost." (The coins were copper.)

1833   (June) The *Volunteer*, carrying 255 persons, mostly immigrants bound for Quebec, ran ashore near Scatarie. (Alexander William Haire petitioned the House for reimbursement for medical treatment he provided for 47 passengers.)

        The *Hope* (tonnage — 454, persons — 143).

1834   (February) The brig *Harmony* (tonnage — 416, crew — 19) was stranded near Scatarie.

The *Montreal* (tonnage — 385, persons — 26).

The brig *Hannah* (tonnage — 309, persons — 16).

The brig *Ranger* (tonnage — 309, persons — 16).

(May 6) Barque *Rebecca* of London foundered among the ice floes off Scatarie. (Six petitioners from Main-à-Dieu who provided the survivors with food and clothing asked the House to reimburse them.)

(May) The brig *Fidelity* under Captain R. Clarke, bound for Quebec from Dublin with 183 immigrants ran aground on Scatarie. Everyone got ashore, but three of the survivors died before being rescued by the inhabitants of Main-à-Dieu. Three passengers were left behind for three weeks, but were then picked up, alive.

The brig *Dove* (tonnage — 153, persons — 12).

The brig *Phillip* (tonnage — 184, persons — 10).

The schooner *Mermaid* (tonnage — 90, persons — 4).

The schooner *Grasshopper* (tonnage — 80, persons — 4).

1835   (June) The barque *William Ewing*, carrying 274 Irish immigrants bound for Quebec was wrecked in fog on Scatarie Island. James Dodd and his crewmen saved all aboard.

Two other, smaller vessels also foundered on the island during this shipping season: the *Joseph & Son* in September, and another (name unknown) in December. The crew of the *Joseph & Son* stayed ten days with people at Main-à-Dieu who petitioned the house to be reimbursed for clothes and food. Two seamen who survived the December wreck were treated for frostbite and had limbs amputated by L.

Grey, Surgeon, of Sydney, who subsequently asked the House to reimburse him.

1836   (December) The brig *Abeona* was wrecked on Scatarie.

[Early in 1837 Charles E. Leonard, Collector of the Colonial Revenue at Sydney travelled to the island to receive duty on the vessel's cargo.]

1838   The *Colombo* foundered near Scatarie.

1840   (October 4) The ship *Sarah & Caroline* of Boston was wrecked. In a notice sent to the *Cape Breton Advocate* her captain made the following statement: "I **Albert Dunbar**, late master of ship *Sarah & Caroline* of Boston, return my most sincere thanks on behalf of myself, officers and crew to J.R. Dodd, Esq., Superintendant of the Island of Scatterie [sic] (Cape Breton) for his timely and humane assistance in taking us from the wreck of the ship *Sarah & Caroline* on the morning of the 4th instant and landing us on the Island at the risk of his own life, and also for his kind and gentlemanly treatment during our stay at his house on the island." (October 12, 1840)

Captain Dunbar was also quoted as saying that he attributed the loss of the *Sarah & Caroline* to an important error in the chart — (an English Chart, he noted).

1841   (May) "The Brig *Breeze*, wrecked on the island of Scatarie in a thick fog, in the Month of May last, and recommend that the amount of £259 12 2 should be granted and paid. The Breeze was bound to Quebec with one hundred and seventy Passengers who were removed to Sydney from the Island of Scatarie after their misfortune and unavoidably detained nearly a fortnight. Their situation was destitute and places of shelter and food were furnished with economy since as many of them as were unable to provide for themselves exceeding one hundred in number were forewarded to their original destination, Québec."

(December 6) ". . . the crew of the Brig *Secret*, wrecked 6th December 1841, in a snowstorm at night on the island of Scatarie — said mariners having narrowly escaped with their lives but with scarcely any covering to protect them from the inclemency of the season." (The *Secret*, 198 tons, was built in Sydney for the Archibalds and, it is thought, was wrecked on her maiden voyage.)

1848   An English brig sank off Scatarie. Its crew were conveyed to Sydney by Joseph Kennedy. The House records state that: "Mr. Dodd (James) ought to have furnished a more full explanation of the facts."

Schooner *John Thomas* built by Samual Brookman, Sydney and sold in 1846 to Michael Kennedy was lost at Scatarie.

1854   (June 9) Schooner *Union* "Healy, Master, of Halifax with a cargo of coal bound from Sydney was stranded on the island of Scatarie on the night of the 9th instant in a dense fog when vessel and cargo became a total wreck."

Barque *Tottenham* bound from Cork to Quebec. Peter Hall Clarke was granted £175 for services to passengers of the wrecked barque: "for waggon [sic] and boat hire and his own personal expenses and services in relation to his superintending as government agent for shipwrecked passengers, the transport of eighty-nine passengers from the place of wreck to Main-à-Dieu and subsequently from Main-à-Dieu to the United States on route to their destination . . .

1855   (July 19) "Brigt. *Balaclava*. Piercy, Master, from Wallace in ballast bound to this port (Sydney) struck on Scatarie in a thick fog on the 19th Instant and became a total wreck — a heavy sea running at the time. The crew were taken off with great difficulty by Boats from the island which came to their assistance immediately after the vessel struck. The Master and the Owner, Mr. McNab, speaks in high terms of the newly appointed superintendent of Scatarie, Mr. James Dodd,* whose attention and kindness were very great; and also Mr. Edward C. Bown,** who was on the island at the time, and who remained on Hay Island (the point where the ship was wrecked) during the night with a boat's crew to protect the property. The vessel drove to sea during the night so that only a small part of the materials were saved."

---

* James Dodd was the son of James R. Dodd who had died in February. He was about 25 in 1855.

** Edward C. Bown was James Dodd's brother-in-law. (On July 15, 1845, at a ceremony at Sherwood, Sydney, he had married Susan Dodd, only daughter of James R. Dodd, then Superintendent of Scatarie).

Appendix G

The following is a list of vessels known to have gone aground on Sable Island during Philip Dodd's tenure as superintendent. It is based partly on the Reverend George Patterson's list of wrecks which occurred during Dodd's residency, published in the book, *Sable Island, its History and Phenomena* (1894). Corrections and additions to Patterson's notations are from Philip Dodd's daily *Journals,* the log of the *Daring,* and the Journals and Proceeding of the House of Assembly of Nova Scotia.

1855 December 7 — Schooner *Primrose*, Captain Myers of Pope's Harbour, from St. John's, Newfoundland for Halifax. (By May 16, 1856, Philip Dodd reported: ". . . there are still in the vessel six pieces of heavy Iron, and which I think had better be sold with the Hull. She now lies high and dry in the sand, and I think could be taken off — but spar and sails would have to be sent for her, as she has nothing standing but her bowsprit, and it is very questionable under the circumstances if she would pay for the risk."

1856 July 2. The American ketch *Commerce* of Charleston, S.C., Captain Hinckley, struck the northeast bar about two and a half miles from the end of the land at about 3 a.m. From Menton for

New York with twenty-five hundred boxes of lemons as cargo.

September 23 — The American brigantine *Alma*, Captain Myles York, from New York. Bound to St. John's, Newfoundland with provisions (beef, pork, flour). Went on shore on the south side of the island about 4 p.m.

December 7 — Schooner *Eliza Ross*, Captain James Muggah of Sydney, Cape Breton, bound for Halifax with a cargo of fish, butter and coals. The vessel grounded on the south side about half a mile off shore below the house of refuge. Too much sea to board until the following morning. The crew were brought ashore in a lifeboat in very heavy seas on December 8th. On the 9th the *Daring* hove in sight, anchored on the south side of the island and put Captain Muggah and his crew on board the *Daring* in a lifeboat. On the 10th Dodd and his men, together with the crew of the *Eliza Ross*, and the crew of the *Daring*, saved the luggage belonging to the crew of the *Eliza Ross* and took off some of that vessel's cargo as well. On the 11th the same men saved all the remaining cargo, with the exception of some dry codfish and coal.

1858   March 19 — Brigantine *Maury* of Lunenburg. LeBlanc, master, with a cargo of codfish, oil, and herrings from Harbor Grace, Newfoundland, bound to Boston. She went on shore about ten o'clock on the night of the eighteenth on the south side near the west end house. Dodd and his men saved the sails of the vessel in the evening at low water. The cargo was salvaged over the next month.

October 26 — The brigantine *Lark* of and from St. John's Newfoundland and bound to Prince Edward Island came ashore on the north side of the island about 8 p.m. in a gale. All hands were saved.

1860	September 10 — American brigantine *Argo* of Bath. From Boston for Lingan, Cape Breton, in ballast. (Captain James Farquhar in *Farquhar's Luck* mentions instead a brigantine called the *Arrow* which was wrecked on the island on this date and all hands lost. Since Farquhar's reminiscences were written down many years after the events, and my source, the *Journals and Proceedings of the House. . .* , was recorded the same year as the shipwreck, I tend to favor the official report.)
1861	April 15 — "At 2 a.m. the American ship *St. Nicholas* of New York, bound to New York, struck on N.E. bar of Sable Island. Got off and was filling so rapidly that the crew had to abandon her in their three boats. The 2nd mate's boat with himself and six men arrived at Arichat and the chief mate's boat with himself and nine men got to Plaster Cove . . . . No accounts as yet of the captain's boat with himself and nine seamen." (Ship was in ballast with a small portion of cargo.) [This report was in Captain Daly's log of the *Daring* — and there seem to be no other reports of this wreck, or information about the survival of the captain and the nine seamen with him.]
1862	May 7 — American barque *Zone*, Captain Fullerton, from Shields, G.B., for Boston, struck on the south side of the northeast bar during the night and broke up immediately. All hands were lost except for one Russian Finlander, John Yanderson, who was saved by slipping his hand through a ringbolt on one of the deck planks, and thus washed ashore. Crew of thirteen all told.
	August 1 — Barque *Jane Lovitt*, commanded by Captain Uttler of Yarmouth, from St. John, N.B. for Cork. The captain and two men stayed on the island. The mate and the remainder of the crew left for the mainland on August 9 in the ship's boat.

1863   July 22 — Brig. *Gordon*, under Capt. Fitzgerald, of
St. John, N.B., bound to Liverpool with a cargo of
deals. The sails, rigging and stores were saved by the
superintendent and taken to Halifax.

August 4 — Steamer *Georgia*, under Captain
Gladell, of Liverpool, bound thence from New York
with a general cargo, a portion of which was saved
by the assistance of the superintendent. The 80
people aboard were saved.

1864   February 27 — Schooner *Weathergage* under
Captain McCuish from Boston to Fortune Bay,
Newfoundland, laden with supplies for the fishery.
She was wrecked on the north side at night. The
crew were all saved and a portion of the cargo.

March 8 — American schooner *Langdon Gillmore*,
of New York, from St. John's, Newfoundland, to
that port with a cargo of fish and oil, wrecked on the
south side of the island at night. The captain and
two of the crew were drowned in endeavouring to
reach the shore by swimming. The remainder of the
crew who remaind on the wreck were rescued by the
lifeboat of the island. The hull broke up a short time
afterwards. None of the cargo was saved, except a
small portion washed ashore.

April 12 — Brigantine *Dash*, of St. John's,
Newfoundland, from Cienfuegos to that port with a
cargo of molasses. She went on shore on the north
side of the north-east bar at night. The crew were all
saved and conveyed to Halifax in the *Daring*. The
cargo was a total loss.

December 20 — "Brigantine *Wm. Bennett,* Capt. E.
Bennett, of St. John, N.B. from Prince Edward
Island for New York with a cargo of produce went
ashore on the north side of the Island at 10 a.m.
Captain, crew and passengers, were all saved by a
line; but two of the lifeboatmen of the Island (Henry
J. Osborn and Peter de Young) after the most brave
and humane conduct, struggling in the midst of surf

during an intensely cold day, to connect a line from the wreck with the shore, upon which the crew and a female passenger with an infant, were safely landed, exhausted by fatigue and cold, perished on their way to their respective stations in the evening. The cargo and hull were a total loss; part of the rigging was saved. The crew remained and were provided for on the Island until the 22nd of March, when they were brought to Halifax by the *Daring*."

1865   March 31 — Brigantine *Triumph*, Capt. Wood, of and for St. John's, Newfoundland, from Figueras, Portugal with a cargo of salt struck on the southeast end of the island and became a total wreck. The crew were saved and provided for on the Island till the 7th of April, when the *Daring* brought them to Halifax.

(June 12) Ship *Malakoff*, Capt. Harris, from Hull for Halifax was stranded on the south side of the northeast bar. The crew were all saved and brought to Halifax. The hull and cargo were a total loss.

1866   February 25 — French packet *Stella Maria*, Capt. Gauthier, from St. Pierre for Halifax, struck on the northwest bar; floated off during the night.

June — Brigantine *Stranger*, Capt. Campbell, from New York for Pictou.

July — Steamship *Ephesus*, Capt. Collins, of Liverpool, G.B., from Norfolk, Virginia, for Liverpool.

August 16 — Barque *Ada York*, Capt. York of Portland, from Liverpool, G.B., loaded with cotton.

August 24 — Barque *Bessie Campbell*, Capt. Lent, of Plymouth, from Newport, G.B. for Portland, Me., struck on the island, and being found to be leaking was run ashore, but afterwards got off.

1867   August — Ship *Rhea Sylvia*, Capt. Roach, of Bristol, G.B., from St. Vincent, Cape de Verde

Islands, for Saint John, N.B.

1868   January — Schooner *Malta*, Capt. McDonald of Annapolis, from St. John's, Newfoundland, for Boston.

June 28 — Schooner *S.H. Cameron*, Capt. McDonald, of Southport, Me., from Banquerall Bank with fish bound home.

The *Albion* lost, 13 men died.

1870   February 24 — Barque *E. Robbins*, Capt. Hilton, loaded with peas. The first mate, Andrew Dunn, and one of the sailors, name unknown, washed off the wreck during the night; the rest of the crew saved by a line.

May 2 — Brigantine *Electo*, Capt. Finlayson, of Charlottetown, P.E.I., from Liverpool, G.B., for Halifax, with a cargo of salt and coal.

Brig *Acton*.

1871   November — Brigantine *Black Duck*, Capt. Landry of and from Québec for Bermuda.

1872   Schooner *Boys* of Gloucester, Mass.

The *Reeve* went down with her entire crew of 23.

1873   March — Schooner *Stella Maria* of St. Pierre-Miquelon.

June — Schooner *Laura R. Burnhan* of Gloucester, Mass.

September 15 — Steamship *Wyoming* of the Guion line, Capt. Morgan, from Liverpool to New York, touched on the northeast bar; got off after throwing overboard £20,000 worth of cargo. Sent a boat's crew ashore for assistance, but sailed away, leaving them on the island.

September 25 — Barque *Humbleton*, Capt. Soreignson of Sunderland, from London for New York.

November 9 — Schooner *Zephyr* of St. Pierre came ashore with four dead bodies on board.

Source Material

The following list represents only some of the sources for this book. Much additional material was derived from old newspapers, manuscripts, letters, family and government documents. Most of these were found in the Public Archives of Nova Scotia (Halifax); the Public Archives of Canada (Ottawa); Archives of the College of Cape Breton, Beaton Institute (Sydney); and the Mount Allison Library (Sackville).

Almon family papers. Public Archives of Nova Scotia.

Armstrong, Bruce. *Sable Island*, Toronto & New York, Doubleday, 1981. (Reprinted in paperback by Formac Publishing Company, Halifax, 1987.)

Bayfield, Henry Wolsey, *The St. Lawrence Survey Journals,* Toronto, Champlain Society, 1986.

Bell family papers. Public Archives of Nova Scotia.

Bollan, William. *The Importance and Advantage of Cape Breton.* New York, Johnson Reprint Corp., 1966. (First published in 1746.)

Brown, Richard, *A History of the Island of Cape Breton.* London, Sampson, Low, Son, and Marston, 1869. (Republished by Mika Republishing Co., Belville, Ontario, 1979.)

The Coal Fields and Coal Trade of the Island of Cape

Breton. London, Sampson, Low, Marston, Low and Serle, 1871.

Brown, Robert R. "Canada's Earliest Railway Lines." Issued by the Railway and Locomotive Historical Society Inc. Baker Library, Harvard Business School, Boston, Mass. Oct. 1949, Bulletin No. 78.

Campbell, Lyall, *Sable Island, Fatal and Fertile Crescent.* Hantsport, Lancelot Press, 1974.

"Sir John Wentworth and the Sable Island Humane Establishment," *Nova Scotia Historical Quarterly*, Vol. 6, No. 3, Sept. 1976, pp. 292-310.

Cape Breton at 200: *Historical Essays in Honour of the Island's Bicentennial 1785-1985,* Kenneth Donovan Ed., Sydney, N.S., University College of Cape Breton Press, 1985.

DesBarres, Joseph Frederick Wallet. *Atlantic Neptune,* London, 1777, 4 volumes.

Dodd family papers. Public Archives of Nova Scotia.

Farquhar, J.A. *Farquhar's Luck.* Halifax, Petheric Press, 1980.

Gilpin J. Bernard. "Sable Island: a lecture." Halifax, Wesleyan Conference Steam Press, 1858.

Grant, Kay. *Samuel Cunard, Pioneer of the Atlantic Steamship.* London, Abelard-Schurman, 1967.

Haliburton, Thomas Chandler. *An Historical and Statistical Account of Nova Scotia* (2 vols.). Halifax, 1829.

Halleck, C. "The Secrets of Sable Island." *Harper's New Monthly Magazine,* 199 (December 1866).

Holland's Description of Cape Breton Island (in 1766 and 1767). Compiled by D.C. Harvey, Public Archives of Nova Scotia, 1935.

Howe, Joseph. "Report on Sable Island." (To His Excellency, Sir John Harvey, Lieutenant Governor of Nova Scotia, Halifax, October 21, 1850.

James, William. "An inquiry into the merits of the principal naval actions between the Great Britain and the United States." Printed for the author by Anthony H. Holland, Acadian Recorder Office, 1816.

[*A full and correct account of the chief naval occurrences of the late war between Great Britain and the United States of America*] . . . London, printed for T. Egerton. 1817.

Johnstone, Caroline Biscoe. *Memories.* Sydney (privately printed), 1931.

Journals and Proceedings of the Nova Scotia House of Assembly (1827-1874).

Legge, J.H. *St. George's, Sydney, Cape Breton.* Sydney, 1970.

Logs of the *Daring*, the *Sylph*, the *Argus.*

Lockwood, Anthony. *A Brief Description of Nova Scotia.* 1818.

Martin, Robert Montgomery, *History of Nova Scotia.* London, Whittaker and Co., 1837.

MacKenzie, Kenneth A. (M.D.). "The Almons," *Nova Scotia Medical Bulletin*, February, 1951.

MacKinnon, J.G. *Old Sydney, Sketches of the Town and its People in Days gone by.* Sydney, C.B., printed by Don MacKinnon, 1918.

Mitcham, Allison. *Offshore Islands of Nova Scotia and New Brunswick.* Hantsport, Lancelot Press, 1984.

Paradise or Purgatory: Island Life in Nova Scotia and New Brunswick. Hantsport, Lancelot Press, 1986.

Monro, Alexander. *History, Geography and Statistics of British North America.* Montreal, John Lovell, 1864.

Murdock, Beamish. *A History of Nova Scotia or Acadie.* Halifax, James Barnes, Vol. I (1865), Vol. II (1866), and Vol. III (1867).

Napier, Henry Edward. *New England blockaded in 1814, the Journal of Henry Edward Napier, lieutenant in HMS Nymphe.* Ed. by Walter Muir Whitehill, Salem, Peabody Museum, 1939.

Newton, Pamela. *Sydney 1785-1985.* Sydney, N.S. City Printers Ltd., 1985.

Patterson, Rev. George. *Sable Island.* Montreal, W. Drysdale & Co.; Halifax, Knight & Co; Pictou, N.S., James McLean & Co., 1894.

Robin, Charles. *Journal of Charles Robin* (1767-1787). (Unpublished). Ottawa, Public Archives of Canada.

Taché, J.C. "Les Sablons," *Nouvelle Soirées Canadiennes.* Montréal, 1885.

Tennyson, Brian. *Impressions of Cape Breton.* 1986.

Uniake, Richard John. *Sketches of Cape Breton.* Public Archives of Nova Scotia, ed., by C. Bruce Fergusson, Halifax, 1958.

Zinck, Jack. *Shipwrecks of Nova Scotia* (Volume 1). Hantsport, Lancelot Press, 1975.

ALLISON MITCHAM

Allison Mitcham is the author of many articles, reviews and poems. She has published eight books, including the best-selling *Offshore Islands of Nova Scotia and New Brunswick,* its sequel, *Paradise or Purgatory,* and *Three Remarkable Maritimers* (all available from Lancelot Press). She has lived in Middle Sackville, New Brunswick for 28 years with her husband Peter. They have three children.

OFFSHORE ISLANDS OF NOVA SCOTIA AND NEW BRUNSWICK

ALLISON MITCHAM

Vivid descriptions of a dozen Atlantic offshore islands take us on a tour from Grand Manan in the Bay of Fundy to Heron Island in the Bay of Chaleur. Information about the history and physical features of the islands is blended with intriguing word portraits of many individuals. "It seems that every island has a ghost. The author describes a midnight gallery of drowned sailors, giant serpents, burning ships and Indian spirits. She has skillfully worked the local lore into the accepted history . . . Mitcham, the poet . . . carries me where I want to go: across the gulf of memory to the Island within." — Harry Thurston, *Atlantic Provinces Book Review*.
146 pages, illustrated with drawings and maps, $6.95.
Available from Lancelot Press, Hantsport, N.S.

PARADISE OR PURGATORY, ISLAND LIFE IN NOVA SCOTIA AND NEW BRUNSWICK

ALLISON MITCHAM

This sequel to *Offshore Islands* contrasts the benefits of independence and peacefulness with the restrictions and isolation of island life. It is a blockbuster, combining diligent research, contemporary interviews, dramatic incidents and fine descriptions of nature. "There are stories of skirmishes between French and English soldiers, of prisoners languishing on islands, of lives of island fishermen and lighthouse keepers, along with a sprinkling of ghost stories . . . a lot of research here about a well-chosen subject." — Bruce Armstrong, *The Atlantic Provinces Book Review*.
225 pages, illustrated, $8.95.
Available from Lancelot Press, Hantsport, N.S.

THREE REMARKABLE MARITIMERS

ALLISON MITCHAM

Scholars and men of action, Moses Perley, Silas Rand and William Ganong personified the new, open-minded mentality of 19th century North America. They were pioneers in the fields of Maritime history, minerology, exploration, folklore and linguistics. "Anyone interested in the natural history of the region will soon discover that these men dominate the scene. They would have had their lives glamorized in movies had they been pioneers of the U.S. rather than the Maritimes," writes the author. Laurel Boone in *Books in Canada* states: "This enjoyable book deserves national recognition and distribution." 139 pages, illustrated, $6.95.

Available from Lancelot Press, Hantsport, N.S.